HIGH-RISK TRANSACTION

The Ryan Coogler - Bank of America Incident

"The Notorious Banker"
James Baca

Copyright 2022 The Notorious Banker, LLC

Thanks to Barbie, Diane and Emmy. Three branch managers who were tough in each of their own ways. I was not always the best teller/banker/manager, but you all know I was always a hard worker. Thanks for the mentoring, and funny enough, this book is for you. We didn't have much resources, but you showed me how to use PRO, my judgment, and my skills.

Thanks to the banking industry for giving me content by being so horrible at times for this second career as a consumer advocate. This side is much more fun to be on!

I tell my teams you get the behaviors that you tolerate!

BRANCH MANAGER OF THE BOFA BRANCH WHERE THE RYAN
COOGLER INCIDENT OCCURRED

NOTICE

Thank you to the Atlanta Police Department for making the Bodycam footage public of this incident which occurred on January 7, 2022 at 1280 West Paces Ferry DR NW in Atlanta, GA.

This footage was recorded by the APD on January 7, 2022 and released to the media on March 10, 2022. It was then aired on many news outlets and still images printed in many newspapers/websites. My use of this footage is for illustration purposes only.

CONTENTS

Title Page
Dedication
Epigraph
Notice
Companion Content For This Book
Preface   1
Who am I, and Why Am I Talking To You About This?   5
The Incident at 1280 West Paces Ferry Rd NW   18
8 Frequently Asked Questions About The Coogler Incident   34
Blame The Teller?   45
Blame The Assistant Manager?   60
Blame The Branch Manager?   77
Blame The Police?   94
Blame Ryan Coogler? (Hell No!)   102
Did Racism Have A Role During This Incident?   109
Did Racism Have A Role In This Incident? (more context)   110
Finally   128
Epilogue   135
Acknowledgement   137
About The Author   139
Books By This Author   141

COMPANION CONTENT FOR THIS BOOK

In order to fully explain my view on the events that occured in Atlanta, GA, I have set up companion content to this book.

The full police bodycam videos of the incident were released to the media via press release by the Atlanta PD. I discuss these at length in the book. I have made the media easily available to you in a playlist I created on my YouTube Channel.

For easy access to the YouTube channel, visit:
http://www.CooglerBofABookPlaylist.com
Hit "Subscribe" while you are there.

In most chapters there are lists of videos with time codes to view to enhance the points I am making and for you to see what happened for yourself, as most of the video was not released on media entities that you may have consumed. I have included time codes in the descriptions of the videos on the channel to easily find the part you are looking for.

For news stories, websites, photos and media content that I cannot share inside the book for copyright and intellectual property reasons that I reference in the book, I have set up a LinkTree. To see what I am referring to in the book, go to the website and click on the link corresponding to that number in the book.

For access to the links, visit:
http://www.CooglerBofABookLinks.com

PREFACE

Thank you for reading my book. Before I get into the weeds here about a topic that is likely to piss off Bank of America, I want to clarify why I am writing this book.

I worked at Bank of America for 13 years. I loved it, except for the days I absolutely despised it. The opinions expressed in this book are solely my own and do not reflect anyone else's that may currently work at Bank of America or any other financial institution.

My commentary is based on the workplace experience I had while at Bank of America, conversations with friends in the banking industry, and discussions with my followers on social media. The mentors I had at the company were important to me in how I improved in my roles. They also taught me to analyze a situation based on the information available and make my conclusions on opinions/recommendations.

During account openings when I was at BofA, a document called an NTT (Note-Taking Tool) had us scribbling notes while talking to a new client to help us draw conclusions as to what products to sell them. This book is a byproduct of my training at Bank of America. I am here to analyze this incident and ensure that both bankers and customers know what went right and what went horribly wrong at 1280 West Paces Ferry Rd in Atlanta on January 7, 2022.

I refuse to take personal shots at anyone involved here. I am merely going to coach their performance in a very tough situation. If I use salty language (Oh, by the way, there's foul language in here), It's just how I write. I will only judge their workplace actions as an observer that was once in banking as a manager and now as a consumer advocate, and that's it. Only God can judge them as people, in my eyes, not me.

As for Ryan Coogler, the victim in this whole horrible ordeal. I hope that if you read this or get wind of it, it finds you well. I loved being a banker and helping people, and I dislike what retail banking has become. Your horrible experience should be a teaching lesson for millions in any service industry, especially banking and police training.

The sensationalism of this story by certain media outlets and commentators without context does no one any favors if we don't address and fix what went on. I wanted to write this book to let people understand how your incident is important on so many levels to so many people. Thank you for understanding.

On that note, I am a "small-business owner" who works hard on my project, *The Notorious Banker*. Creating content on social media to help people understand big banks is important to me. Helping people navigate through bank issues means a lot to me. I want to write 100 books about banking if I can. This one came out of nowhere, though. I am excited to write, but I hate that the content in this book happened to a human being, celebrity or not.

So with that, aside from expenses in the cost of labor, production, distribution, and marketing of this book, yours truly, James Baca, commits to donating a healthy portion of the net proceeds of this book to good causes local and nationwide. I don't want to reap crazy profits from another person's bad experience. That makes it sound like I am a banker again. I want to help people, which I love to do, and I feel this book will help.

In the last couple of years, I have used profits from my project, The Notorious Banker, to donate to local food banks in my area. Two of them near and dear to my heart.

Casa de Peregrinos in Las Cruces, NM where in the last two years since COVID, I have seen so many of my old BofA customers (My old branch is two blocks away) coming to the food bank to get free groceries, because times are tough for them. I know from my relationships with them that they weren't great Pre-COVID as well.

Also, I donate to Aggie Cupboard on the campus of New Mexico State University. College students don't always have a ton of help. Some have families to feed, and need a little help to feed them while getting through school. I'd rather give them this food that take out student loans for such a need. I try to donate as often as I can with proceeds from my project.

Donating tons of food to people who need it, people who

I remember as customers of my bank, is something that changed my outlook on life. If this book hits and is successful in people reading and reacting to it, I will be so happy because it means people will be helped and informed. Please follow my Twitter Account @BankBetterGuy for details on where I will donate any proceeds of this project. I want to make sure my bills are paid, which at the moment they are, and the rest can go to people who need it.

James

TikTok: @NotoriousBanker (1)

Twitter: @BankBetterGuy (2)

WHO AM I, AND WHY AM I TALKING TO YOU ABOUT THIS?

I woke up at 7 am on Wednesday, March 9, 2022, just like I always do. I stay up late the night before because I plan out my weekly shopping as an extreme couponer. Wednesday is always a foggy day for me. I roll out of bed to get my cell phone and check Twitter for any bank news which may have happened during my sleep. My project focuses on bank news and policies and how they impact people at risk.

Loading up my Facebook inadvertently, I saw a headline by TMZ that would make me work 10x as hard this week. "Black Panther Director Ryan Coogler Wrongly Targeted as Bank Robber." (3) There was a photo of Ryan Coogler in a hoodie and hat. His outfit screamed comfort, not bank robber to me. The crazy headline screamed something else to me. I muttered under my breath, "Bank of America." There was no mention of the BofA in the post until I clicked through. I just knew it beforehand.

One of my favorite podcasters and writers has always been Bill Simmons. He inspired me to write in a humorous "like I am talking to you in my living room" way, and his podcast inspired me to do my podcast, <u>The Notorious Banker</u>, since 2018. He has one "theory" that I have co-opted and stolen for my work. He has something called the "Tyson Zone."

The Tyson Zone (4) is named after Heavyweight Boxing Champion Mike Tyson. We all know that he was the most dangerous man ever to step foot inside a ring. What we also know is that his lifestyle outside the ring was insanity. Whether it was his marriages, owning tigers, wrecking his sports car into a tree, or biting the ear off an opponent in one of the biggest fights of my generation, there never was a story involving Mike Tyson you couldn't believe.

You could say, "I saw Mike Tyson at In-N-Out Burger with Dr. Dre, and he was singing a Dolly Parton song," Based on past experiences, you would believe that person who told that tale. The Tyson Zone states that no matter how wild the story is, you are likely to believe it because it included Michael Gerard Tyson.

The Tyson Zone for Bill Simmons is the Bank of America Zone for me. I muttered under my breath, "Bank of America," because I knew without reading it that only Bank of America can create a shit storm so insane over nothing and causes them to eat it on social media for weeks on end. It's literally in their nature. They are the Dick Van Dyke flipping over the ottoman of banks. (Is that too dated a reference?)

I click on the TMZ story. Sure enough, Bank of America thought that Ryan Coogler, famed director of "Black Panther," "Creed," and many other excellent movies was potentially a bank robber. Someone in the financial center (don't let BofA hear you call it a 'branch') chose to call the cops on him for being "suspicious." This incident is the most incredibly dumb thing I have ever seen BofA be a part of, and I have been affiliated with them as a client or employee for 17 years. Bank of America triggered this for absolutely no valid reason.

The Ryan Coogler story hit home to all the people who loved his films. It also hits home to all the people who share the same skin color. It also made people think that if it can happen to Ryan Coogler, "Man, this can happen to me too."

This story has consumed my month, and the only way to expunge it from my brain is to write at length about it from a different perspective than you might have heard from other places. I promise you this book will give you unique insight into why this happened, how it happened, and what's to stop this from happening again even tomorrow? Why should you hear from me about this topic? I will get to that in a bit. Let me first do something that no one else on social media, YouTube, or the written word has done.

I want to apologize directly to Ryan Coogler. Why? Because I think this moment, which is undoubtedly one of the worst experiences of his life, is being dissected so that it is likely uncomfortable to discuss. I find it notable that I could not see any social media pages for him, which is unique for such a high-profile person in Hollywood. I don't think it is a bad thing. Trust me. It's helped me calm down since I started using social media only for work purposes only after March 11, 2020. I get it because of the toxicity of conversations.

I apologize to Ryan for even having to mention his name or mention the people with him. As a former banker, I apologize to him as a customer for disclosing that he is a Bank of America customer. I was trained at BofA that if a kid walked past his mom in the financial center and the kid asked me, "Is my mommy a customer here?" I was trained to say, "Unfortunately, I cannot disclose that information due to privacy concerns."....to a fucking kid!

I apologize to Ryan Coogler on behalf of myself, James Baca, for being a part of the branch banking machine and what it has become. When I was at my last full stop in banking, all the things that changed, many of which were on full display at 1280 West Paces Ferry Road in Atlanta, the site of the incident on January 7th, were altered to impact the customer experience. The goal? To make you even less known to the people who, in the case of Ryan, called the cops on him. In my new line of work, I am told upwards of 50-75 times a day how bad Bank of America, Wells Fargo, and others are.

I apologize to Ryan Coogler for writing this book, having to use his experience as the example to write the book I have dreamed of for nearly five years, and to use it for the benefit of my family and me and my growth as a small business owner. If it were

John Henderson IV, Diane Smythe, Lori Doyle, or any other person that this happened to, with what I know from this incident, I would have written this book as well.

It fucking sucks that the only way I can get my point across is when it happens to a successful person when it happens all the time to others without the success of Ryan Coogler. I am not knocking his success. I praise it, and I envy it. The man is younger than me, and he is so talented and awesome. I hate that his horrible tale is the story I have to hitch my wagon on to have this discussion in a book or on social media.

Jeez, I apologized to Ryan Coogler more than Bank of America ever will and with 100x the sincerity. More on that in this book.

Who am I, and what am I doing here? Let me finally fill you in. My name is James Baca. I am a consumer advocate, workplace advocate, and the host of a podcast called *The Notorious Banker* (5), which breaks down issues with big banks, stories from my past, and I have discussions with old coworkers, customers, and others about the state of big banking now. I have established a social media presence on Twitter and TikTok. However, days after this incident, Bank of America got my TikTok account suspended for talking about the Ryan Coogler incident and sharing the police bodycam footage on social. I appealed and got it back a week later. Suck it, BofA. Follow me @NotoriousBanker on TikTok because BofA hates it!

I have a side gig giving help to people with bank problems. Do you have fraud on your account through Zelle or someone stealing your account number or debit card, and your bank isn't helping you? I strategize to get you help, including leaning on my media friends I have made in the last five years and drafting comprehensive letters on your behalf to people who can actually help you. I teach people how to talk to bank management to get the point across more emphatically and efficiently to get things fixed the way they want. I don't teach people to lie. I show them how to properly tell the truth.

My workplace advocacy is more about informing people of their rights as employees, mainly in my state. At Bank of America, I was shamed anytime I had to take a leak, much less drink a sip of water. I think bullying employees is the most significant product Bank of America produces, with excessive checking accounts a close second. I have helped a couple of businesses settle disputes with their employees, which has allowed for better work environments. I get paid to do these things. How cool, huh? No real training at all, and I get things done.

I have Bank of America to thank for bank product knowledge, policy knowledge, and interoffice politics. Thank you, Bank of America, for training me to listen, look people in the eyes, take ownership of a situation, and do all the things they do to oversell clients on accounts at a level that makes Wells Fargo look like girl scouts hawking cookies. They also trained me in finding out who REALLY is running the show at the branch level. (Hint: branch managers are figureheads. They are the Maytag repairman of the financial industry)

They taught me that meritocracy is not on the menu, successful employees get stuck, and mediocre employees get praised and moved up the chain. They taught me that you can be called worthless, even after hitting 150% of your sales goal the last quarter, because you didn't open up one account from 9 am-10 am on the Wednesday before Thanksgiving, and "We have to question your commitment to your job." Yep, that was me for years.

My career at Bank of America began on December 7, 2005, when I was hired as a part-time 20-hour bank teller while still in college. It was one of several jobs I had during my time there. Part-Time Teller, Full Time Teller (there's a difference beyond just the number of hours you get), vault teller, teller supervisor, sales and service specialist (half teller/half banker), personal banker, relationship manager (sales), all while being a trusted supervisor in my branch the last several years.

My end date at Bank of America was August 17, 2018, when the consolidation of bank branches in my area led to the closure of my bank, the agreement to severance pay for all of my branch teammates, but not for me. Instead, I was told how "important" I was to the company, so I was promised a transfer to another BofA location. I felt honored by that, so much so that I turned down a $60,000/yr managerial job at a rival bank and a better paying job at a bank across the street from my branch because I was loyal to BofA.

On August 13th, 2018, I found out how disloyal they are. My bank accused me of an "error." I had helped a client from Indiana named Stephanie. On May 3, 2018, she went to my branch to open an account. She had 2 IDs and a check from her job waiting tables at a local restaurant. It was a $28 check, I believe. Anyway, we get to talking. She has a black eye. She tells me that she left an abusive boyfriend back home a week prior, and she and her friend landed here in New Mexico. Pretty deep conversation for a bank chat.

I enter her ID info and address and fill out all the stuff I need on the computer to get an account open. I paused every couple of minutes because it was a good chat. Some would say it was an excessive chat. But I got the account done, and I helped her at the ATM deposit her check, and I never saw her again.

Cut back to August, and BofA Investigations informs my boss that on the person I helped, I created an error that could end up getting me in trouble. Indiana Drivers Licenses are ten numbers and are formatted like this 1234-56-7890. Two hyphens in the number. BofA is claiming that I omitted the dashes in entering her number on the system, and because of that, they are of the thought that this Stephanie isn't even a real person.

The dumb thing about that? When typing in a specific state's ID number, the computer system pre-fills in the dashes for you, so I couldn't do what they accused me of doing. Anyhoo, long story short, because of a $4.95 monthly fee incurred by the account I opened up for her, it was considered a "performance loss," and I was summarily fired over the phone by my manager Christy Vargas for it. Over $4.95 after 13 years of working there, never missing a day of work due to illness, and on the last day my old branch was open, I canceled an anniversary vacation with my wife to be there to help them close down my location.

Bank of America never paid me for vacation hours accrued that I couldn't use because they wanted me there to close the bank. Bank of America burned me out of my Q2 2018 bonus for sales, being one of the top salespeople in the region working for a branch that wasn't going to exist. I did home loans, home equity lines, credit cards, and accounts for people who wouldn't have that location. I was that good. Frankly, they owe me money.

But like my mom once told me, "When someone owes you something, and they don't pay you back, you make sure they never fucking forget you." My mom is not in the mafia, although it wouldn't surprise me if she were. But she still is a 5 foot nothing 110lb spitfire, still at 61 years old. There'll be a book one day which will include how my mom got a subprime home loan from BofA before I worked there on a $9/hr salary and how it demolished her credit ever since. Does 2008 ring a bell to you all?

The one thing I was always good at while working for Bank of America was showing clients how the sausage was made. I was tired of being yelled at for what that company did to people. I walked people through complex processes, not unlike what should have happened to Mr Coogler during his request, to show them that yes, even them, one person out of 67,000,000 clients mattered to this company and, most importantly, to me and my branch. I had a ton of loyal customers, some would make appointments to ONLY see me, waiting hours at a time to interact with me, and that's what made me great at sales there.

My direct manager Christy resented it because I was supposed to be there for sales and not to be their friend. But in developing the bonds with my clients, my ex-branch manager Barbie, myself, and our other supervisor, Stacie, made that a model branch the last few years we were there because we didn't lie to our customers the way THEY (corporate) do.

So when I left BofA, I immediately thought that I was freed from the corporate chains and took my hand to social media and walked people through issues they were having at BofA and Wells, where I was a client. I informed clients about the actual policies of banks, how to walk into a bank with more knowledge than even the person in charge, and to get things done on their terms. I was successful. My Twitter account, @bankbetterguy, has helped thousands of people since I started my project, now known as The Notorious Banker. Use the hashtag #vigilantecustomerservice on Twitter to see my handiwork.

I help people with things big and small. I did it all, whether getting a $12 fee refunded, informing customers how not to incur reg D penalties, or walking people through the bumpy mortgage processes that big banks put clients through. The mortgage process at BofA was also something that, as a client, made me temporarily homeless for a week while managing a BofA in 2016 (A story for another book). I helped a professor in the city of Atlanta, where Ryan Coogler was screwed over by BofA, get his $800,000 mortgage finished [6] when Bank of America refused to help him close the loan after a 3-month process. Love ya, Dr. V! Because of that interaction, I am familiar with the area where Ryan Coogler was detained and the bank's hierarchy in Atlanta through my work.

During COVID in 2020, I can safely say that was my most successful time doing my Notorious Banker Project, which in a way, is the saddest fucking thing ever. I have seen banks hurt so many people. All the things I saw made me feel compelled to help. To be fair, COVID brought out the best in some businesses and the worst in others.

Bank of America, in a press release [7], allegedly committed to working with customers on fees that impacted them while they were out of work or sick during COVID. With 4-6 hour hold times on the phone, not many people got help. Then in the fall of 2020, they trained associates on how to deny those fees and communicate the message to the client. BofA and Wells Fargo also "temporarily closed" branches using COVID as the excuse, with some branches still being closed today. Some banks are still closed even though mask mandates are mostly gone in the US, and cases are way down.

Is it a coincidence that the branches "hardest hit by COVID" enough to "temporarily close" are in low-income neighborhoods or communities of color? Branches that I know from my time at BofA to be super busy remain closed. One of the main reasons is that those branches are heavy on service requests and not heavy with many high-dollar revenue-generating customers who get revenue-generating products. Some branches have no ETA on when they are reopening STILL two years later.

Read the weekly OCC report (8) as I do. You will see that BofA permanently closes many of those temp-closed banks after shooing away all the business. Cross-check those in the weekly report by googling the address, and you'll see the branches never reopened. It was a sly way to get rid of some underperforming (in terms of sales) branches. Couple that with pushing repeat "low-revenue generating" clients, ones that my old boss used to call "sales cloggers," to ATMs and the app and away from other branches where they impact the sales goals of bankers.

Bank of America closed a branch in Gallup, NM, (9) near the Navajo Nation, which I knew in my time there to be the busiest branch in the region. Why? Because nearly all the Natives that live there are on the poverty line and get one measly monthly check a month, a client that BofA hates because there is no growth. So they just up and closed, leaving the closest branch to the Navajo people 2 hours away (10), leaving only ATMs in the community with no place to get financial guidance in a world with $4 gas where these folks make $700/month in income. Closing this branch impacted a lot of people.

I helped over 30 businesses go through the PPP Loan paperwork hell that BofA and Wells put them through to stall them from getting it through in time before funding dried up. That was a struggle, but I got it done with my sheer effort. I made enough money in "consulting" to keep me afloat for a year. People were so amazing to me. Here's one man's story of what he went through because of BofA (11).

One of my biggest successes is helping people deal with issues regarding their unemployment benefits during the pandemic. What did I do? I coached people on how to fight for what was rightfully theirs effectively. Many people had their states giving them shit. You would be surprised how many people gave up on getting benefits. It was a labor of love to help them fight.

I worked hard, most notably in California, where billions of unemployment money was lost due to fraud. Bank of America, a company paid to run the system, was freezing out the cards of clients not accused of fraud who rightfully were entitled to their benefits (12). The bank did this to mitigate potential losses while impacting several hundred thousand people. It was bullshit. I did several interviews with reporters who were digging into the news (13) to basically tell them the m.o. of how I believed fraud happened, and how the bank handles victims of the bank's poor fraud protection.

My battles were also fought with Wells Fargo, which runs the unemployment card racket in New Mexico. I had to help certain people impacted by the freezing of their benefits on their debit cards issued by Wells on behalf of the state. You can include me in that, as I had to fight for my money. I detailed my year-long journey to fight for my benefits in a book I wrote called *PLEASE TRY YOUR CALL AGAIN LATER* (14).

I care so much about helping people, and I have pieced together a meaningful living doing it. It's not as fruitful as selling an old lady a 5th credit card, but it is honest work. I make up the difference in money by donating blood plasma 2x a week for about $700 a month more income. I pay my bills on time, and I am about to pay off my student loans. I am living the American dream, though not with money or possessions. But happiness.

I got a great wife, a great support structure, and a skill that almost no one else possesses. I take on big banks and their BS with my followers, and I WIN! Big banks hate me, and while I will likely never work for one again, I feel I have a lot to give to retail banking. I hated how banking beats you down mentally and rarely builds you back up.

I have many stories about my life there, but I will save those for another book because I am here to talk about the man of the hour, Director Ryan Coogler. I will intersperse some examples of how I can use my past at that company to clarify what happened at the Bank of America on 1280 West Paces Ferry Rd.

Here's the thing: I was a teller. I was also a very fucking shitty horrible teller when I started. I don't think I would have lasted six months there if it wasn't for people quitting all around me. I couldn't balance my drawer; I think I ended my teller career at 90% balancing accuracy, which means one day out of every 10, I lost the bank money. You don't get fired if you are above 88%. I couldn't understand bank policy, and mainly I pissed a lot of clients off. I was the spitting image of the teller in the Coogler incident. Trust me. But unlike her, I got better, I learned from my mistakes, and I asked questions to make sure I got more efficient, and it took me from $8 to $25 an hour in 5 years at that company.

I was a supervisor. I was a shitty supervisor at first, too. I didn't know how to communicate news to clients well. I got yelled at constantly. I took a couple of losses that I should've known better. I wanted to be friends with tellers instead of their supervisor, which got me in trouble. Then I matured, became better and more efficient.

I finally became a manager, and I was a shitty manager at first, too. I didn't realize that when you get the title "manager" at BofA, you don't really manage anything, and in fact, there are 9-12 "managers" above you, so you are handcuffed from doing anything they don't tell you to do. I hated it. I asked my boss to remove my job title from my business card because I wasn't really a manager. They denied that. But then I got better and made my branch efficient and customer friendly. Then they closed us down because we were on the poor side of town, and we were all fired, including me, without BofA paying severance and other monies owed to me.

I learned to make lemonade out of lemons there and to save the peel to eat it to lower the high blood pressure that fucking company gave me. (I googled that fact about lemon peel) But I learned how things REALLY work, and the branches are not there to help you. If you are not opening accounts, bringing money into the bank from another firm, or looking to buy a home, car, or invest, you are in the fucking way in a branch. $12,000 withdrawal for Ryan Coogler? It was someone's pain in the ass at that branch for many reasons that I will discuss. They see Ryan as taking two people away from hitting their sales goal. Their sales goals for the quarter had just started that week he showed up.

It's crap, but it is true. Bank branches are there not to give you your money, cash your check, and give old ladies calendars and free pens. Nope, they are there to make a multi-billion dollar bank more billions, and when they are done maxing out a neighborhood, they will leave you without the resource of a bank branch and financial advice. Think of the alien/ locust analogy that President Bill Pullman references in _Independence Day_, another great film. The banks are like locusts. They consume all the resources in an area, and they move on. Pretty good reference, eh?

Ryan Coogler was a problem to Bank of America simply for wanting his own money. Was it also because he is Black? Yes, and I will reference why in the coming pages. This case has more branches than young Forrest Gump and Jenny can swing on. I am here to break it down from the teller side, the supervisor side, the manager's side, the police side, the rest of Bank of America you don't see on the video side, and of course, from Ryan Coogler's side. I will give you more context than anyone else because I was the banker forced to act horrible to customers by our policies. I am also a brown-skinned man who experienced poor customer service at the same bank.

Millions can talk about this. Me? I lived it in many ways, except I wasn't stupid enough to call 911 on a customer who presented all the identification I could handle to do a transaction. I am doing this book so you can focus on the idiots who messed this up in Atlanta and the whole company who messes up like this daily.

THE INCIDENT AT 1280 WEST PACES FERRY RD NW

If you have seen this story, you don't need me to do a full recap of what went down at 1280 West Paces Ferry Rd NW in the Buckhead section of Atlanta, GA. You bought this book because of the what, and you are here for the why! I get that. But let me just set the scene a bit, and we can get away from reciting the facts repeatedly.

On Friday, January 7th, 2022, Ryan Coogler, acclaimed director of "Black Panther" and "Creed" currently filming the sequel to "Black Panther" inside of Tyler Perry Studios in Atlanta, went to a Bank of America branch for a cash withdrawal of $12,000. Bank of America refers to this kind of transaction as an "electronic withdrawal."

He presents the teller Erica Glass with two forms of identification. Coogler used his debit card at the Quick Service Terminal (QST) at the teller window and entered a PIN. That is considered a valid form of identification minus your ID up to $5,000 at a BofA window. He needed $12,000, though, so protocol states that a second form of ID is necessary.

HIGH-RISK TRANSACTION

He presents his California ID. Valid forms of ID in his case to take that out would be State-Issued Driver's License or ID, US Passport or Visa, Military ID, among others. He had that.

The NY Times, in their reporting (15), got the steps/facts slightly incorrect in writing the story. I don't mean that the way it sounds. The reporters who discussed this likely never worked at BofA, so the way it plays out is different that how they laid it out. It's hard to explain the steps to someone who never was a teller for a big bank in the 2000s and beyond. The reporters did a phenomenal job and their allusion to the teller police interview sent me on a deep dive. It's just that the steps mentioned after that couldn't happen the way they did because there are different processes than what the average bank client knows.

The NY Times stated that Coogler presented a withdrawal slip for $12,000. That is incorrect. Bank of America, from at least 2004, when I started banking there, to the present day, does not have "withdrawal slips" for its clients at the check-writing station.

BofA has what I refer to as "counter checks," which act as a defacto withdrawal slip, but usually only for a bank purpose like moving money into a new account set up by the client or purchasing an official item such as a cashiers check or money order, though Bank of America retired money orders during the time I was there. There is no slip Coogler would have filled out to initiate the transaction.

Now since there was no withdrawal slip, it makes Ryan Coogler's note with instructions the main focus of her attention. According to the interview by the police with the teller, Erica Glass, he inserted his debit card, a normal process, and then presented a note on the back of an in-state deposit slip. The teller mentioned in the interview with the police. I can identify that it was a deposit slip as well. Ryan Coogler's note says, "I would like to withdraw $12,000 cash from my checking account. Please do the money counter somewhere else. I would like to be discreet." (16)

19

I was going to post a photo of it on here, but it has a TMZ watermark, and I don't know about copyright issues and fair use and all that. If you have the eBook, click the link above. If you have a paperback, go to the URL provided at the beginning to see the note.

From the note, it tells me that this is not an irregular transaction from Ryan Coogler as he is aware of BofA processes, and we will get into why that matters in this book. According to the teller in the interview, she asked for his ID, which would be the California ID I had mentioned. She hits "w" for withdrawal (I always said the MerlinTeller system they have is idiot-proof. Boy was I wrong.) and enters in the amount.

The New York Times wrote what happened next: *The teller "received an alert notification" from Mr. Coogler's account and quickly advised her manager that he was trying to rob the bank branch in the Buckhead section of Atlanta, the report states.*

According to the teller, she mentions that once she hit w for withdrawal, the screen locks up with a "red box" message indicating it was a "high-risk" transaction. The way NYT refers to it makes it sound like the message was the catalyst for accusing him of robbery. How the teller mentions it, she is well-aware of the "high-risk" notification, and she knows her screen is locked until a supervisor can complete the transaction for her, which usually means the supervisor, who we now know as the assistant manager will do due diligence before approving it.

The way the teller at this moment is going about it is something that would appear to be normal to Ryan Coogler's naked eye. Even if he only did this 5x ever, I would say 4 of those times, a teller needed to excuse themselves to get their supervisor's help. That is more an indication of what the teller limits are at the location he's at more than anything. There is almost no way a second person would not have been involved in previous times.

So, Ryan Coogler likely knew he would have to wait because

a CTR Form for doing transactions over $10k in cash inside a bank also needed to be done. Any decent supervisor knows how serious the report is at BofA, where you must make sure you correctly enter in all CTR Forms for high dollar transactions. They document your ssn, ID number, account number, amount, transaction type and verify your address and occupation. CTR entry is a tedious task, and I am unsure of the teller since she was newer and had a much lower limit than the rest of the associates ever had to do a CTR before.

    Before excusing herself, she says she mentioned to Coogler which account he wanted to use for the withdrawal. Since the note said, "checking account", I would assume…checking account. But here's one bone I will throw Bank of America's way. If Ryan has more than one checking account, which is pretty likely because of his wealth and relationship at Bank of America, the teller may not know which one, especially if multiple checking accounts have more than the amount requested. So when she states, "out of which account?" he says, "Look at the note," according to her.

    I can see where that would bring confusion if he had multiple accounts. A more seasoned teller would have checked on the service side of the software to see which checking account is directly linked to the card he inserted.

    She says she goes to excuse herself to get her manager, again to me, a very normal part of the transaction, so in a sense, nothing has gone "wrong" yet. When she goes to get her manager, who is the Indian man in the video, the teller tells him that she doesn't feel comfortable with the transaction because, as she says to him, "he just handed me a note, saying to 'look at the note.'" The teller mentions that the assistant manager wants her to go back out there with him so they can talk to Coogler about his transaction. At that point, it is an acceptable way for the assistant manager to handle the associate request. I have been in both roles, and it is infrequent that the teller can articulate the whole story to where the assistant manager makes assumptions based on that story.

What the teller says after he requests to go back out there is something that is not acceptable from a banker's perspective, both from the fact that she is disobeying her boss and, of course, the soon to be happening phone call, refused to go back out there with him, stating that "I'm pregnant. I don't know if he has a gun or whatever."

Funny enough, even if she got the request and everything wrong, and he only wanted to take out say... $1,200, the assistant manager would still be needed to cancel the transaction. She can't just cancel out of that at that point. BofA puts a spot where a supervisor has to clear your mistake, similar to what you will see at a store where some manager comes with a key. There's no "key" at BofA, just a password from a supervisor.

Glass, the teller, then mentioned she called 911, and the assistant manager allegedly also called 911. I can't verify her claim with any released media from the City of Atlanta. The only 911 call that exists is hers online (17), and there is an issue with that, mainly because of how quickly she called 911 without going through the proper protocol.

She mentions in the call that Ryan Coogler was just waiting around in the same spot this whole time while all of this was happening. Meanwhile, from the looks of the bank, as the police arrived and handcuffed Coogler, it looks like the whole bank, aside from the teller and her supervisor, was unaware this was happening. Even the other people on the teller line are doing regular transactions while this is happening. That is the most bizarre part of it for me.

No matter how discreet Ryan Coogler wanted to be, I believe it is almost impossible for them to be discreet based on BofA protocol. You would be amazed at how everyone listens to everyone else's business, especially in the teller area. To be fair to Bank of America (Wow, I am saying that), the transaction by its nature is not discreet because it requires at minimum a second person to complete it, and also, that person who is helping the teller is going to be researching to prevent losses, matching signatures and such.

Bank of America protocol creates that spectacle mainly because, let's say that there are tons of people waiting in line to be helped, and this whole transaction needs the supervisor to complete it. When people in line get to the 10-minute mark in waiting, they start to stare in your direction when you are a teller and, by extension, eyeballing your client.

According to the interviews with the manager and the teller via police bodycam, Ryan Coogler, was asked several times during the process by people walking around the bank who are called "lobby leaders" by Bank of America if he was being helped. The implication was that they were a part of the stall technique to make sure Ryan Coogler was unaware of the police were being called on him.

This scenario that the employees crafted seems far-fetched because human nature will dictate that if the person who cheerfully is asking Coogler if he was being helped had the information that it's a potential bank robber with a gun as the teller mentioned, would that person armed with only an iPad and bullshit fake smile and cheer go to the front lines to keep Coogler at bay? That leads to a ton of other questions as to protecting people at that point. It's simply false.

So, after police go into the teller area with guns drawn, an understandably confused Ryan Coogler, standing and waiting with his legs crossed, is looking at both cops, which is the scariest part of this incident. His brain is not telling him, "Oh shit. They are here for me because they think I did something." Think about the best "Candid Camera" moments to the best TikTok pranks. The person is dumbfounded about what is going on, making it funnier. There was one problem, though.

This shit was most certainly not funny. There are two cops with guns, confused glares by Ryan Coogler, and a confident knowledge in the cops' minds that "This is the motherfucker who is robbing this place!" and with Ryan Coogler, there's likely a thought in his mind of, "Oh, Shit. I wonder who they are after. I need to make a move out of here."

What happens if he moves to the exit because Ryan Coogler thinks a criminal is in his midst, not knowing that they believe it is him? Unanswerable questions that are being answered by a lot of people who have seen a lot of bodycam footage recently. The police role is up for debate on how it was handled. They had exaggerated information from the teller given to them by dispatchers, and they were understandably thinking they were walking into a potentially high-risk situation from their perspective.

They tell Coogler to put his hands behind his back, and one officer slaps cuffs on him. Coogler is then led out of the fucking cavernous bank and to a nearby police car. I just want to add that branch looks like an old Southern courthouse. Instead of Bank of America being there, it seems like "To Kill A Mockingbird" should be performed there.

Two officers escort him to the car, and he is then questioned by several officers outside. What we didn't see when the video first came out and didn't learn until later that day that it was released was that two people inside the car Ryan Coogler was riding around in were also detained. An African-American man in his 30s or 40s and an older lady, possibly in her 50s and 60s, who we come to find out in Ryan Coogler's interview as his "Baby's Nurse." When they are talked to by cops, they are equally as confused as Ryan Coogler is as to what the hell is going on.

So while they are questioning Ryan Coogler, he asks the policeman to look at the badge on his hip, which is a work ID identifying him as a movie director. I wasn't sure where the badge was from exactly. I assume it is either a pass from Tyler Perry Studios where he was working, or possibly it was a card from the DGA, Director's Guild of America. Coogler states, "I got a badge on me. If you run my name, you can understand why you should take off these cuffs. If you can not do it, it's going to be really bad for you. Just google it (my name)."

The arrest is an uncomfortable part for me because I understand where he is coming from at this moment. Coogler is blindsided by being taken into custody. He's in handcuffs for something that wasn't possible to be accused of a few minutes ago, and I think people who are genuinely innocent of any crime like him assert how not guilty they are of anything.

After researching who he is, he is seated in the police car. He asks the police to take the glasses off his face because he feels like he is going to have a panic attack, and they oblige. Coogler then asks if his "Baby's Nurse" is being detained, which the cops confirm is the case. The frustration and sadness on his face, as he is told, are evident.

HIGH-RISK TRANSACTION

The cops then ask him, "Did the officers explain what is going on here?" and Coogler says, "Not really. I heard someone say that I passed a note." The cops said they got a call that Coogler was trying to rob a bank based on the note that he passed the teller. The police officer asks, "Can you tell me what is going on?" Ryan Coogler then states that the money is for a medical assistant (baby's nurse) that works for him and prefers to be paid in cash. He then says, "Every time I make a withdrawal, it's a large amount. If I don't write on the note how much I want and that I don't want it run (through the cash counter), because I don't feel safe."

At this point, this confirms to me that he has done this multiple times before just based on that statement, I'll get why this is necessary to assert blame fairly later in the book. The police, after his explanation as to the transaction and the note say, "That's the reason we are out here because we don't exactly know what is going on." The confusion is evident with the police officers, and there is a note of frustration in their voices because it seems at that point is all a big misunderstanding.

They uncuff Coogler and let his party go from detainment, and Coogler continues to talk to the cops about the situation, and he asks where the phone call came from, and the cops respond, "It came from the bank." Coogler gets more upset at that point, which you can tell by the inflection of his voice.

The cops then offer unsolicited financial advice on how Ryan Coogler should bank, which irritates me. "Have you ever considered speaking to them before you make a transaction like that? Have you ever considered talking to someone about what you are trying to do?" Coogler responds with, "Every Bank of America I ever went to in my entire fucking life, this never happened. You are saying (what I did wrong) from your perspective, and you have guns and vests. What about my perspective?

She never said it was a fucking problem. I asked her if that was going to be ok with her. She said, 'Yeah.' I put my own card in, put my own PIN in, she asked to see my ID. I gave it to her, and she went to the back. People keep coming out (saying), 'Are they taking care of you?' ….next thing, I hear fucking glocks!"

Coogler gets more and more worked up, understandably so as the conversation goes on. He then documents all the badge numbers of the cops on the scene. In a video that has not been seen by many of this incident, the police are with the branch manager as she "personally apologizes for any inconvenience" to Ryan Coogler directly, gives her a business card with her name, the assistant manager's name, and the teller's name and gives her manager's name and info as well. That part is BofA protocol. I have never seen them basically out the name of someone who made a mistake like that.

While that is happening, the questioning of the teller is going on. She mentions how she sees it from her perspective and how Ryan Coogler was "weird' and not talking to her. She mentions the note and states that she asked for an additional ID and confirmation of which account he wanted to use to make the withdrawal. When the high-risk message pops up is when she left, which even in a typical transaction is fine by me, but she asserts to her assistant manager that she doesn't feel comfortable and states that she called 911.

The cops ask her, and she confirms that his information is still on her screen, and then they read the note back to her and state, "Well, it sounded like he wanted to be discreet." The teller then says, "I didn't say he was trying to rob me," which the cops then say, "NONONONONONONONONO. We get that. I mean, I kinda like how you do it a little bit, because you never know.". Forgive the commentary, but at this point, they have to know that she fucked up right then and there.

Teller then says, "I'm not accusing him of anything." The police then asked her to go to her station and unlock her computer so they could match the name on the screen with the identification that they had with them. She then confirms it is "Ryan Coogler" on the screen. They then excuse themselves.

On the bodycam, the two police officers discuss the incident, and one of them says, "It's legit." the other states, "Yeah, everything looks legit," while discussing the same reason Ryan Coogler gave about wanting discretion for his transaction. It seems like they get it. I just figure those police officers who are around crime all the time in a big city like Atlanta would understand the pitfalls of someone openly flaunting a big chunk of cash around.

We didn't get complete closure in any of the videos that show if Coogler ever got his money. However, towards the end of the video, where the manager is apologizing, it sounds like she wanted to help him and "run the transaction personally," which is technically impossible for a branch manager. The whole incident lasts roughly an hour, but indeed, behind the scenes at Bank of America and the Atlanta Police Department, I am sure there are reports galore about this incident, and they are likely still talking about it at Bank of America. I can only hope that this book sparks another conversation about what happened there.

This story was released to the public on March 9th. I am

unsure who broke the story, who asked around about it, or if Ryan Coogler mentioned it to someone, and that's how this all came to light. I know I first saw it on TMZ on Facebook, which posted it at about 6 am Mountain Time on Wednesday, March 9th, and then it blew up from there. The Atlanta Police Department put out a press release with about 5GB of Bodycam footage, which ate up a lot of my data plan on my phone, along with the 911 call from the Teller. It was time and data well spent. I have seen this incident from every angle, and with my bank expertise, I know how to analyze better than most what the teller and manager did to cause such a stir.

The Twitterverse took it over. I discuss Bank of America stories regularly on social media, and I have never seen a story take over quite like that. Everyone talked about it, including well-respected commentators who chided Bank of America for this horrible incident. My Twitter account received over 3 million impressions, my Tiktok videos were in the millions, and I added about 5000 new followers to all my social media channels.

My Tiktok is monetized, and let's just say I was able to pay my utilities with the money generated from this. In a perfect world, I'd prefer to make my money some other way. I hate that banks hurt people, which gives me content that I'd rather not have. What this told me though is that a LOT of people cared about what happened here.

The Ryan Coogler incident is unique, though. It's an astoundingly big story that hits pop culture, race, big bad banks, and how bad customer service has gotten. It was the perfect storm of shit. A week later, it is still buzzing on my social media channels. My fledgling YouTube channel has seen a 50,000% increase in views, and I have tripled my followers there. It's amazing how much time the internet devoted to this story.

Deciding to write about this one incident was difficult for me to approach because Bank of America put out a public apology to Ryan Coogler, which said, "We deeply regret that this incident occurred. It should never have happened, and we have apologized to Mr. Coogler." Ryan Coogler said, "This situation should have never happened, and Bank of America worked with me and addressed it to my satisfaction. We have moved on."

The problem with moving on for Ryan Coogler and with Bank of America, which rarely publicly apologizes like this, is that shit like this still happens every day at Bank of America and other big banks. Ok, maybe not a false arrest and a famous person being taken into custody because of an allegedly hysterical Pregnant woman who thought Ryan Coogler was a bank robber. I mean mistakes, profiling, policy enforcement that has their roots in discriminating against people they don't want in the bank.

I don't just mean discriminating against Black people like the opinion of most people who are mad at Bank of America because of this. It's more than this. I mean discriminating against people who want to do the most basic transactions. Banks see a customer not going in there to get a new product impeding them from selling new products to others. Service has gone way down since banks, always sales-focused, became even more so in the last several years, ignoring customers with simple requests.

COVID paused sales goals, which halted growth at Bank of America at that level of banking. The other arms of BofA more than propped up what retail banking couldn't provide after a bumpy 6 month period in 2020. With less foot traffic, there was less opportunity to create new business. BofA has many branches "temporarily closed" as of March 2022. I think COVID is the excuse they are using as justification, why some banks aren't open, although case numbers are down across the board, and mask mandates and stay-at-home orders are a thing of the past.

Fine, I will believe them at face value, although it seems like there were 100 news stories last year about branches mysteriously being closed (18). The PR machine at Bank of America put up the same fucking cookie-cutter statement as to why they were closed all across the country as if Americans hadn't heard of a thing called Google. They indirectly reference prioritizing the health of their clients and staff, while in the same statement, vaguely referencing that employees may not be available because their family has COVID.

I wouldn't doubt it if I didn't see the same statement in different publications in different communities I talk to people who worked at these temporarily closed branches. Some of them contribute to my project monetarily because they believe in what I do to help people.

Why do I know these things happen? Because of those people. Because I went to work every single day, and I put in 13 years of employment at Bank of America. In a world of many talking heads, my giant head had as much individual transaction experience as anyone at that company while I was there. I cared about my job and, most of the time, my former company.

I did over a quarter of a million teller transactions in my tenure there, which included thousands of withdrawals for various amounts, both big and small. I know every pop-up that can happen, every ID acceptable under BofA's acceptable ID list. I understand how the customer "role play" training I was given taught me how to correctly identify risk and continue to help a person instead of calling the cops on them for being "Weird," as the teller mentioned. I know from hard work. I know from conversations to this very day with people I know at BofA who tell me how things evolved since I left.

The following parts of this book will discuss why certain people are more at fault than the others in the branch. I also will break down some frequently asked questions that I have replied to about 38763 times since the incident happened.

I also want to tell you why we need to step back and review all the facts we know with all the things I will say to you, and you can make your own decision on who's most to blame. It's easy to send people to the guillotine without understanding what got them there. It's the mentality we need to stop having. This book exists because there is so much nuance as to why everyone sucked at this BofA branch.

Playlist Viewing For This Chapter:

Video #1 (911 Call) In Full

Video #3 (Coogler Arrest) 5:00-8:00

Video #5 (Coogler Interview) 6:00-23:00

Video #4 (Teller Interview) 6:00-16:30

Video #6 (Manager Apology) 36:30-41:00

8 FREQUENTLY ASKED QUESTIONS ABOUT THE COOGLER INCIDENT

There are many things we can disseminate about the case. But certain media outlets and many people got specific processes wrong, so I decided to do this chapter to clarify some things I DO know and dispel factually incorrect items.

Why did he write that note? Didn't he know that you can't write notes in a bank?

The note thing is one of the things I hated hearing the most during this situation. "You can't write notes in a bank" is the most ridiculous thing because, as a former teller, I would say that 1 out of every ten clients writes a note to the teller, explaining what they want to do. The vast majority of those people usually represent businesses, and the notes are change orders breaking down the denominations. Every teller has a "shred bin" where most of the paper that lands there are customer notes explaining transactions. The bank bags those notes and locks them in a huge bin. If they ever need to locate something from a specific day, it's easy to find as the date is labeled on the bag.

HIGH-RISK TRANSACTION

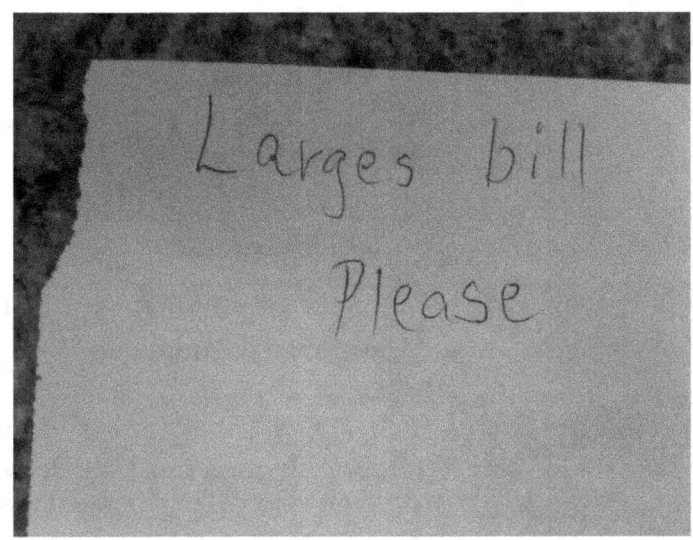

For context, in my 20s, when I was a teller, we would take photos of the funnier notes we got from clients. Whether it was notes that had poor grammar, misspellings, or just funny ones, we documented them with our phones. Of course, I broke the rules having my phone out, but I did it. I got older, wiser, and more professional from that time, but I will be the first to say I was immature and dumb. I still have 100s of photos of these "notes" though.

I had deaf clients, mute clients, people with social anxiety disorder write notes to me. My spanish-speaking clients would have their English speaking kids write notes for me to understand their request. Notes are fine. Are they used in robberies? Yes, but so are getaway cars. Are you going to ban people from driving to the bank?

Bank protocol would be to keep the robbery note if it was an actual robbery, if it was safe to keep it. You were to give it back to the robber if they asked for it. I just don't understand how the teller NEVER got a note before that incident. That's a 1 in 100 chance that was the case.

If you arrested everyone who ever gave me a note in the bank, I would have sent the equivalent of an NBA arena crowd to jail. It's literally that many people and that many notes over the years. Yes, you can't yell "bomb" in an airport or "fire" in a movie theater, but the paper is acceptable in a bank as long as the note isn't a robbery note, just like spray paint is OK to buy as long as you aren't tagging neighborhood walls with gang propaganda.

Why didn't he write it on the withdrawal slip?

Trick question. There are NO withdrawal slips at Bank of America. Everything is an electronic withdrawal. BofA carries what some would call "counter checks," which are typically internal use only for cashier's checks or debiting one account and crediting another account. I have only seen one branch ever have those available to clients at a station because I believe people were trying to use them as checks outside of the bank, and there is no way to process those. Some smaller banks give counter checks like that to clients when they have a smaller processing footprint. BofA doesn't do this

There's a receipt called an electronic withdrawal slip, which for more significant amounts, a client signs and is given a carbon copy receipt of the transactions. Those slips that are signed are filed and retained. There's a ton of tracking and auditing on those things, and it's likely Ryan Coogler knew the process from past transactions, which is important to note and adds to why he had a chill demeanor while waiting for his money.

It should be on the record that the note he wrote was written on a deposit slip, which at a regular run branch would be frowned upon to use those things as scrap paper. BofA makes the branches buy their own supplies like they are fucking Herbalife distributors and get mad at management for ordering too much stuff. Isn't ordering a lot of deposit slips because you need them a good problem to have?

What does the teller mean that it was a "high-risk" transaction?

After becoming a banker and manager, Bank of America

added a prompt on the teller screens when whatever algorithm they used detected an irregular transaction for that client and dubbed it a "high risk." That means that a supervisor or a teller with authority over themselves needs to do additional research to complete the transaction.

Typically, if a transaction requires a signature, you would use your computer to match the signature on old checks, signature cards, or other documents. If that isn't available, then you can ask for a second form of ID at that point if needed. You check your computer to make sure the IDs given to you match what you have on the system. You then document all the ways you identified this person in the red box on the screen, and the supervisor enters their name and password to complete the transaction. In theory, with this extensive method of IDing, the customer, the branch, and especially the teller and supervisor can't take a personal loss which could lead to termination. It would be considered a "policy loss."

I will say, as a man with supervisor authority over the tellers because of the way our branch was staffed, I fucking hated this red box high-risk warning for a multitude of reasons. The main one was the impact on wait time. It hurt because I usually was busy opening accounts, and my branch manager was busy with her stuff. So for a teller to stop what they are doing, wait for a moment to interrupt her or me to get that override, us having to do the extra research and approve it, it can be 5-10 minutes more. It pisses off the client wanting to get this done, the people in line behind them, and the customer I left in my office unattended to do that override for my underling. It was bullshit and probably cost us money by impacting our customer satisfaction scores.

Also, I hated it for our clients because our client base, for the most part, was not unknown to us. I would put "Known to associate" on many things I did because I got to know these people personally. I used to get in trouble for using that dropdown so often. Well, what the fuck? I knew these people.

So when this red box warning popped up, you had to ask for 2 IDs from someone who knows about you and your family personally, talk sports with, see at the store. It's like Bank of America's way of saying, "Whoa, customer. We should not get too close." because it makes the associate seem like they never can honestly vouch for the person they see all the time.

The bank says it's to prevent losses, but I can tell you stories of victims of in-person fraud where these checkpoints were blown right through, and BofA still refused to pay the clients back for their mistake. You can see my work on my Twitter account [19].

There's a racial element to this high-risk message because it often happened in my branch to customers we knew well at our branch. My branch was nearly 100% Hispanic, with half of the clients speaking primarily Spanish. A lot of long-term employees disliked the high-risk warning when it started. The high-risk message wasn't specific to Ryan Coogler, as I have seen it thousands of times. It could have been triggered based on the amount, where his account was domiciled (California), where he was located with the California account (Georgia), and the irregularity of the transaction relative to their account history.

Didn't they know he was a celebrity?

This one will be fun to answer because I get to share a story about one of the best friends I ever worked with in branch banking. The answer is no. They don't know he's a celebrity just by bringing up his screen at the bank. Unless you know who he is, it will not tell you. That being said, I have dealt with many famous people in my time at Bank of America. I had an NFL veteran that lived in my hometown and went to school with one of my assistant managers. He's a nice guy, and I respect the life he made after football.

I had a former manager of the Toronto Blue Jays as a regular client. He was funny as hell to talk to, and I think he enjoyed coming to see me. I had one former world boxing champion, whose name I will say because he passed on. Long live Johnny "Mi Vida Loca" Tapia, one of the best boxers that true boxing fans love. Finally, one of my other clients was a musician from a Grammy-Award-winning group. He had gotten his start in music in my hometown. Since then, he has become well-known and even sold his song to Bank of America and Target for their commercials. A quick google search will tell you who I mean.

I knew those people, and they have varying degrees of fame. Still, when you help someone at Bank of America of almost any notoriety, they have an alert they send to your bosses that you helped someone famous. They investigate to see if you had a legitimate business reason for bringing that person up. If not, there is hell to pay: write-ups, even termination.

I lived in fear of that alert, which I will rename out of respect for BofA. Did I really say that I respect them? Let's call it the "Damian" alert. It's a play on what it is called. I feared it because two customers who regularly came into my bank were Michael Jackson and Michael Jordan. Seriously. One of them is a very successful college coach, and the other is just a regular guy. But when you would search for them on the screen when helping them, many people with those names come up, including possibly those famous ones. If you accidentally hit Basketball's Michael Jordan and exit out without context as to what happened, your ass is grass.

The mayor of my city of Las Cruces, a man who owned an insurance office next to my branch, was considered one of these "famous" people, and my managers got an alert every time I helped him. He was next door, for god's sake! Plus to me, a mayor isn't famous in a town of 100,000 people. I see him at the basketball games all the time. If you were an NYC resident and you saw Eric Adams at your Starbucks, you'd flip out! It's more rare than a small-town mayor!

The bosses don't tell you if you got this "Damian" alert unless they find you didn't have a legit business reason to look them up. That leads me to my friend and ex-coworker Omar. He and I were great friends, and he's the only man who can make me laugh out loud still to this day. He got fired in 2013 for the horrible, disgusting task of helping his mom make a deposit using his computer, though he was the only teller on duty. There was no way for her to do her business other than going through the teller area and utilizing him, but the bank disposed of him.

Two or three months before that, he got a "final write-up" because he used Merlin Teller on one of the more boring days to search for Marshall Bruce Mathers III, also known to the public as rap legend Eminem. Of course, with a name like that, he was likely the only person to come up on the screen, so the bank threw up a "Damian" alert, and my boss got wind of it, and he almost lost his job then.

He didn't steal money or do anything but just bring it up on his screen. I will not defend him because you shouldn't do that, but that's how hardcore BofA is about protecting their "important" people, aka the rich.

Love you, Omar.

I turn into Grampa Simpson when I try to make a point. Sorry for being so long-winded and telling stories in the middle of chapters. My point is that even if Ryan Coogler's transaction had gone smoothly, this "Damian" alert would have happened behind the scenes. BofA corporate security would then have analyzed the transaction to ensure it was legit and done by him, not an impostor. The bank would have had all this research behind the scenes because of the prominent person who did it, even if it was a tedious non-eventful interaction. It was someone's problem even before the situation at the bank occurred to make sure the banks he visited complied in helping him.

After this news came out, I can almost guarantee you that some bank employee somewhere is having a long talk with their boss at Bank of America for unauthorized access to Ryan Coogler's profile based on this news that happened with this incident. Some looky-loo searched it and is likely not having a fun time at work now because of that damn "Damian" alert. To answer a question people may have, yes, your profile always sticks around even after leaving the bank and closing your accounts, which I am sure he did. Celebrity doesn't buy you any favors at the bank, I guess?

Since he is famous, could they have called someone to vouch for him?

Yes, more than likely, although I don't think the employees were thinking rationally with how fast things went down here. Now, I don't believe this because he is famous. I think they could have vouched for him because he's rich. When you are rich at Bank of America, you are likely under the umbrella of Private Banking or Merrill Lynch. I believe one of the phrases they used to use was "wealth management." So what happens when you have a shit ton of money with that company, you usually have someone assigned to you.

I've gotten nasty emails from people on the Merrill side asking me why I did certain things for their clients. They are that client's "personal" banker, so we can't touch them. I once had sales credit for a home loan taken away even though I helped the wealthy person make the application. But since he was assigned to a wealth management person, they got credit for my work, which was stupid.

Does that "vouching" work all the time? No. Some managers still won't help with certain things even if someone is identified as a BofA associate through an internal channel. They have a system where they generate a one-time use code to identify a current employee. Some managers will ignore that way of helping because if there is a loss to be taken, it's on the person doing the transaction, not the person vouching for the client. But as I said, there was no rational thinking here.

Why did he want to be discreet? Doesn't that make him look more suspicious?

Because Bank of America's policy and procedure on acknowledging customer requests and counting and paying out cash is anything but discreet, I got yelled at hundreds of times for not saying the customer's name three times in one teller interaction. Sometimes it's hard to stuff the name into a chat 3x when it only takes a minute to do something. BofA also wants you to confirm the transaction three times. It's also said to alert the manager for overrides/cross-selling/whatever. So the bank would want the teller to say loud enough, "I'LL BE GLAD TO HELP YOU, MR. COOGLER! YOU WANTED TO TAKE $12,000 OUT, MR. COOGLER. SURE THING. OK, MR. COOGLER, PLEASE CONFIRM YOUR TRANSACTION FOR $12,000 FOR ME PLEASE. THANK YOU. OK MR. COOGLER, $12,000, 1, 2, 3, 4…."

That is acceptable per their protocols, and nothing short will get "coaching" from your boss. I got those coaching moments. Coogler mentions in the police video the need for discretion, simply for the possibility of "jugging," something BofA employees are taught during training. Some criminals are trying to see who gets out a lot of money and then either attack them in the parking lot and rob them right then and there or follow them to another location for the robbery to occur. Jugging is serious, and it does happen in many areas, including in my sister city, El Paso, TX, a few years back.

Bank of America would never say that it is wrong how goddamn loud and repetitive they want to make their employees sound during the transaction, that they might be to blame for potential jugging. Heaven's to Betsy, no! They feel that in their hearts, the way they do things has no bearing on how crooks attack clients. (wink) How we communicated with clients is something I railed against while employed there. The sound of 120 $100 bills through the money counter can be audible to the whole bank and turn heads. Ryan Coogler knew that, so he wanted them not to do that.

I have taken people, famous and not, to my office to count the money with the door closed for privacy. Bringing people into an office for privacy is normal and not weird to anyone who has worked in banking, even for a few months. Some people are just paranoid, understandably so. Since the teller is technically a relationship banker, which allows her sales access and service access to customers and probably has access to an office in the branch, she had the easiest path to make his discretion request happen.

Should Ryan Coogler Sue?

I hate this one, too, because it's so nonsensical. Does Ryan Coogler have a case for a lawsuit? Probably. But the vast majority of my social media posts say that he should sue the teller directly. For what? A judgment she can't pay, and he'll never get? Will he pay legal fees and retainer fees to a lawyer for a court to make a judgment on the teller and just take the monetary loss? Stupid. I don't think people understand how lawsuits work. He could sue the bank, which employed her, and maybe he will get a little something out of that, but suing her is dumb. You can't get blood out of a turnip, and you can't get money out of a person with a low-income job who lives in an expensive city like Atlanta.

Bank of America wouldn't necessarily like the PR nightmare it would have from defending itself in this lawsuit. It can open up a whole can of worms that they don't want people to see and have the Elizabeth Warrens and Katie Porters of the world on their balls all the time about these horrible business practices they do.

Sue the cops? You really can't here because they only knew what they were told, which was wrong, and you can't fault them for doing their job. Some people won't like that, but if he was arrested and sent to jail, maybe thrown down on the ground, perhaps something could percolate. But the cops were fed bullshit, and they had to act accordingly to what they knew, which was all a lie.

In my opinion, Bank of America will quietly settle with Ryan Coogler. In a couple of weeks, you will see some big charity donation that won't necessarily be tied directly to Coogler (meaning they won't mention that it spawned from the incident) to some charity he supports.

Just FYI, people, lawsuits take years sometimes, and from the looks of the statements Ryan Coogler and BofA made, they just want to wash their hands of this shit.

Why did it take us 2 months to know about this?

Simple. I am sure the police were investigating what was going on in regards to what went on at Bank of America and quite possibly were in the middle of perhaps settling a claim from Ryan Coogler on their actions on that day. I also think BofA was likely doing their internal investigation of all the things their associates did that day, which included film from their cameras. The TMZ story had the angle of Coogler from the teller area perspective, which is not on any police footage, as well as a clear photo of the note he wrote for his request. I feel that BofA cleared the use of those things after doing what they needed to do with the investigation.

I think whoever got fired/disciplined has already happened, and any potential legal settlements have been done; otherwise, we wouldn't have a wealth of info and video to peruse about this case.

So there you go. I think I answered most of the questions I got on social media. I am sure I missed one, but oh well, who else is doing a book about this? No one in the purview, so ha!

BLAME THE TELLER?

It seems so easy, right? After hearing the 911 call and seeing her interview with the police, you can comfortably assume that she is likely not a MENSA member. The consensus slam on her is that she is not bright by the tone of her voice. I will avoid cheap shots like that because I want to be fair. It's a hard job, no matter what people say. She caused all of this, though.

But what if, for a brief, fleeting moment, I tell you that while she is most definitely the most to blame for calling the cops on Ryan Coogler and causing this drama that has caused me to write a book, she only shares part of the overall blame and I refuse to 100% pin it on her. Don't throw this book away yet. Let me explain. Ok? Ok.

First of all, let me just state her name once more. Her name is Erica Glass. Now I will be referring to her as "The Teller" from here on out. Why? Should we repeat her name ad nauseam to train everyone to know the horrible things she did? No. I don't believe in that. I've been cyber-bullied before, and it is not fun. I have been mocked online in every possible way, which is not fun. I am not religious but hate the sin but love the sinner. The woman lied, or I guess you can say, misled the 911 operator, her boss, and the police as to what went down.

But that doesn't mean I am going to keep saying her name. I am saying it here because it was on the bodycam footage, and that is technically public domain, much like the press release the cops put out.

I mentioned before how we just like to blame everything and everyone for things that happen. In a bodycam video, the manager blamed the teller with the lazy excuse, "She's new. She's not seasoned" Ok, fine. It makes sense in many ways, but it doesn't absolve the bank from a shitty policy.

Being a teller is the most demanding job I have ever had. It is more than just counting money. Many things can quickly derail your career path. Balancing accuracy can be challenging for some. What about being judged on your speed? What about how many times you call the customer by their name? How about the ability to warm transfer referrals for sales to bankers, watch out for people trying to defraud you, and of course, relevant to this incident, be aware of your surroundings and your situation to prevent robbery or any crime. It's a lot, trust me.

They also find ways to keep you in check to stunt your growth in the company. That means finding new ways to "coach" you. I once got a verbal write-up for hitting the F11 button too many times. Seriously. You are treated like shit. The pay was ass a long time ago. You are expected to prop up the branch with sales referrals for people making 4x more than you who have better training and sales skills than you. Plus, they got all the bonus money anyway, so there's nothing in it for you except your hourly rate.

It's not a job for everyone. I worked with over 100 tellers in 13 years at Bank of America. Some were good, some were horrible, and some remind me of this teller here in the Coogler case. I worked with a girl named Yesenia, and I swear, she's the Hispanic version of this teller personified. We were friends, so I say with love that she shouldn't have fucking worked there and stopped doing so a decade ago.

One of the reasons Bank of America has upped its pay recently to $25/hour in 3 years is that they know that they aren't attracting top talent at that level of banking, which is a problem. People with excellent skills realize they can make as much or more money at a better job, where it is not as taxing as BofA. You sometimes get less than qualified candidates when you have a weak talent pool. With that pay increase also comes added responsibility, though, something of which I found out while writing this book and watching the police videos—more in a bit.

So there is some validity to "she's new" as an excuse from personal experience. I was a fucking miserably bad teller when I first started. I couldn't manage my cash efficiently. I had a hard time learning all the command buttons. Plus, BofA emphasizes using 10-key for many of their cash transactions, which I never did until I worked there—coupled with being shy, making mistakes, and causing my tiny branch to have long lines because of my incompetence. I know how it feels. My manager at the time, Emmy, decided not to fire me, which I still don't get to this day, but of course, I am thankful for it.

So being bad is par for the course when you are new, but there are obvious things I saw during this incident that make me question why it even happened.

First off, when you are "new," you are 99.9% sure to have low check cashing/withdrawal limits, what BofA calls "Freedom to Act." When I started 15 years ago at BofA, my transaction limit was 500 bucks. When my last branch hired our final teller, her limit was 1,000 bucks. It's not a lot of money at all.

When you try to do a transaction for more than your limit,

a pop-up shows up with a name and password box for a supervisor to enter their info after they approve your override. The pop-up screen with a supervisor override needed is a screen there is absolutely no way she never saw until meeting Ryan Coogler. Even if they set her limit at $2,500, if she was a teller on the teller line for a month, she likely needed 20-30 overrides minimum. They are also in a more affluent neighborhood, so it's possible that she's seen it even more than that.

The manager would have had a hand in that transaction anyway. He would have interacted with Ryan Coogler himself during that interaction to "complete" the transaction had it gotten that far. Her assistant manager would take care of the override for the "high-risk" box that she mentioned in the video (more on that in a bit). Also, he would have likely attended the final part of the transaction after counting the money. Because of the amount of money withdrawn, a CTR form needs to be completed immediately after that transaction. Tellers usually enter them, and supervisors approve them.

A CTR (Currency Transaction Form) is a form that banks do to report to regulators any transaction involving more than $10,000 in cash with a customer. It requires inputting information, including date of birth, social security number, transaction type, ID information, and even job title. It's part of banks' AML or anti-money laundering programs. It's a fucking serious offense not to input one in the system when helping a client for that amount.

You could even lose your job, and it hits the performance metrics of the branch itself for having a CTR "Defect." I have never seen a branch empowered to let their tellers handle such transactions, mainly because most didn't have the teller limits to complete a $10k+ transaction. That's why little things like this are essential to this incident.

Her interaction with a direct supervisor should have been much more polished than she claimed it was. The system would have prompted her no differently. There's something broken with that relationship because if she were so new, the supervisor would be hovering around her to ensure she was doing things correctly on the system. That's part of training a teller even when actual "training" is finished.

Training is another animal. Jesus. The last ten years of training at Bank of America have become horrible. I can only speak up to 2018, but in 2012, when I became a banker, they flew me out to Dallas, and I learned in person in a classroom setting about real-world problem-solving. I was told I was one of the last bankers to get that in-person training. It was actually awesome. Even in 2005, my teller training was mainly working with a more experienced associate at a window to get the keys right, along with confidence in interacting with a live person. In-person interaction made me better.

(I always wanted to note in a book that I eventually wrote that while Bank of America was generous in paying for a flight, hotel, and meals for my training in Dallas, they were cheap asses in other ways. They told me they couldn't rent a car for me and that I should be fine getting to my training, as everything is within walking distance. My hotel was 2.3 miles away from the training center in Addison. Let's just say after 5 days of having to walk dangerous city streets near the Dallas North Tollway, where cars were whizzing by at crazy speeds, I know that Dallas isn't pedestrian-friendly, and Bank of America was just cheap. I seriously thought I would die getting hit by a car.)

Something about that training made a lot of associates I worked with for a long time good. Right around 2012, the same year I was dodging pickups in Dallas, BofA changed all banker training and teller training to virtual learning. Virtual learning was a foreign concept at the time, but of course, since COVID, all of your children have become adept at this type of learning. After 2020, most Americans are aware of virtual learning.

The training is shit, though. It felt like a Yahoo chat room mixed with exercises brought to you by ABC Mouse. It was not intellectually stimulating. Your managers put you on an off-site computer, usually in another room for 3-6 weeks as you take all those courses, and never interact with your teammates in the branch, just more bored trainees in other parts of the country. It's weird, and it seems like when they were "ready" to go on the teller line, they had to re-learn how to really do things because some of the scenarios in training were just not realistic.

That is also a critical factor in what happened here. Being new has a lot of disadvantages as a teller these days because every branch, every client base is different, and it takes time to know the flow of your financial center to spot something wrong, like someone robbing the bank.

I have never been in a bank robbery in all my time there, but the teller I replaced back home in Socorro, NM, quit her teller job there because of a robbery. She was robbed two years in a row by the same woman who wore the same Halloween mask. The woman was caught the second time, but that terrified the teller who quit, and through all that, I ended up working there two months later. What a weird coincidence that someone's irrational fear is how I got a job there.

If you were aware of your surroundings and did your job right, you wouldn't have had that fear inside of you. God, I sound like these BofA creeps that I worked for, but they have a point. An efficient bank branch has lobby leaders, these people walking around the lobby with iPads greeting you as you walk in the door. Some people think they are Walmart-style greeters, but they are there for two reasons.

The first is to ask you what you are doing there to see if they can identify a product to sell you and check you in to see a banker or confirm you have an appointment. Think of it as a bank version of a conversation of how a man tries to turn every conversation with a woman into one about sex. That's what they are trained to do. Everything becomes a sales conversation.

The other reason they are there is a simple one. They are there to make eye contact with whoever walks in as an indirect way of dissuading people from robbing the bank. Pretty ingenious, huh? Are you going to rob the bank if some fake cheery person says, "Welcome to Bank of America! My name is James. How can we provide you with excellence today?" Probably not. The Ned Flanders routine is going to knock most robbers off their game. Okily-dokily?

That extends to the tellers as well. You are supposed to make eye contact if there is a line to identify your customers and let them know you will be right with them. It acts as a way of breaking up the length of time those poor souls are waiting. Bank of America has whittled tellers down to 1 in many locations, even on busy days. I have heard reports of managers not scheduling tellers for part of the day in some locations, which fucking blows my mind.

Eye contact also acts as the same deterrent for "robbers." Again, robbers are not likely to rob if you burn a hole in them with your fake cheeriness. My BofA bosses would like this point I am making simply because I was guilty of this, too, because it took me years to make that direct eye contact with people without getting embarrassed.

If corporate security saw no eye contact while Ryan Coogler was waiting his turn, this is likely a sticking point for BofA in how the branch handled it. I am sure they ran through all the security footage to see who interacted with him to determine whether they broke protocol and then overcorrected when she started "feeling uncomfy."

The most egregious error that she made, which can get her fired, to be honest, was how she got around to calling 911. From what I gathered from what she said to the cops, it looks like one BofA protocol was skipped in calling 911. You are told that you trip your silent alarm if you feel uncomfortable with a situation or feel like you are in danger. There are buttons/pull tabs at every teller station and some offices. But all associates carry around a handheld alarm. It usually has two buttons and only triggers while in range when you hit both buttons simultaneously.

Did she not do that? I think she didn't because her training would have told her to hit those buttons if she were uncomfortable. That would have triggered SOACC, which is BofA corporate security. They would have called the branch, and if no one had answered, they would have called the cops for her, and I guess Ryan Coogler likely would have been in handcuffs again. Sigh, but it's true. That's what was missed, in my opinion. Bank employees are trained to do it this way.

Even if you call 911 immediately and don't call SOACC directly, you should trigger the alarm. It's just part of the process. Some things didn't add up. Did she tell her supervisor that she was going to call 911? Did she tell her supervisor precisely what happened the way it happened? She claims she did, but we don't know that for sure, only hearing her account on the interview recorded with the police bodycam.

You don't do things the way she did without theoretically putting your team at risk. I know she was trying to protect herself and her baby, but what about the other tellers, bankers, clients, and others in the vicinity? Was she going to leave them to fend for themselves if Coogler wasn't Coogler and was a brazen bank robber with a gun?

Let's discuss the 911 call. So when you hear the 911 call, you hear the teller mention that her manager had told her to call the police. Still, in the police interview, she mentioned that she told her manager what was going on and that he wanted to go talk to the customer, and she refused, saying, "I'm Pregnant. I don't know if he had a gun or what.", and she mentions that she stayed there and called 911. That's a considerable inconsistency and leads me to believe that she tried to pin her supervisor as the person who greenlighted her to call the cops, which is problematic and technically insubordination.

The assistant manager sounds like he's following protocol here because he was trying to complete the transaction for the client. I guess what I am trying to say in so many words is that the assistant manager was not afraid of the interaction based on what the teller was telling him. She mentions the note, and he still wants to see the customer based on her words, although she doesn't want to so she can protect her child.

The increased emphasis on the note in the call sounds all the more comical, the more you hear it because other than that, it sounds like the 911 operator is already not buying this is a serious call. However, she still dispatches police to the scene regardless. The 911 dispatcher even says, "Well, maybe he just wants to be discreet." She mentions on the call that there are two other tellers out in the lobby helping customers. She also says she is "afraid" to check on them for fear of whatever. I just don't understand what the hell is going on.

From the looks of where she called from after seeing a mini-layout of the building, she could easily spot the tellers in her line of sight. There are not a lot of places for her to hide. She is fluffing up the severity of the incident as the call goes on. The way she handled it could have led to disaster at that point. I think this is where grounds for termination are, in my opinion. It's almost akin to "Swatting."

I don't know if you have ever heard of this phrase, but it's something your kids likely know about or know someone who has done it. Swatting happens when these kids, who play video games all day, develop unhealthy anger towards someone online. The kids then use 911 to play a prank, usually stating the person they are targeting is holding his family hostage and will kill them if they don't get to (the target's address) immediately. This shit happens often, and people have died due to this "prank." The teller's exaggeration made this another level of police involvement than was needed, even if Coogler was some person committing fraud and not someone putting the bank in danger, in my opinion.

I am a 38-year-old man, so this next part is not fun to write for me, but I have to say it. I have seen many pregnant women at Bank of America work there until the day they popped out their children. The empowered women I worked with at the branches I worked at were incredible to me and gave this author more respect for women in the workplace than I never knew I had. That being said, the bank manager treats her like she is a total invalid, as if her condition precludes her from making a rational decision. If I were a woman, I would be offended.

Bank of America, in March alone, over celebrates National Women's Month by posting all these facts on their social media about women small business owners and how many women work for Bank of America. Even if it's not genuine sincerity based on how I have seen women treated there, it's nice to make the post honoring those women in the workforce. Although I disagree with their statement of how many women are in leadership roles, I can say that I worked with mostly amazing women in my time there. They need to be treated better at that company.

When her manager talks to the cops walking in to interview her, she portrays the teller as this fragile little thing who may not be able to handle a difficult conversation. That should piss off many women who see it, especially if you have been pregnant before. Right around this time, they feel that nothing is going on here, and the cops just want to clarify some stuff in their interview with the teller.

But the manager is now worried about the physical/mental well-being of the teller, which to me, sounds a little funky. The branch manager was likely in contact with her boss and SOACC on how to handle this. Suppose the teller was a discipline problem before. Maybe the manager was afraid of the teller filing a hostile workplace report or something. Because, no doubt, people are getting yelled at behind the scenes, and this is the manager's concern? Wasn't a "robber" just in here? I don't buy it.

HIGH-RISK TRANSACTION

I mentioned earlier that I have worked with a teller like her who just refused to help certain people do certain transactions. It was not based on bias, but "I don't feel comfortable. I am not going to take a loss. I won't do it for you." I often was the teller who had to help the now pissed-off client take care of what they needed to do. This same teller I worked with refused to withdraw money for a client of ours, one the rest of us knew, simply because he didn't look like his driver's license photo. He had a giant bandage on his head from skin cancer surgery, and his face was puffy.

The teller here made me remember that flashback, and it pisses me off to this day. It wouldn't surprise me if she were looking for a reason to have been "freaked out" to take a leave of absence before her 3-month maternity leave and then quit. I mean, hell, I have had coworkers get a doctor's note to stay home before maternity leave, and they openly talked about it with us as their friends. I am a male, so I will never experience those feelings, so I can't empathize the way someone who can get pregnant can. I am talking about the physical part, but I understand it's a challenge to be expecting a child and work at that damn place.

Everything just seemed a little too amped up to 11 in this Ryan Coogler situation for it to make any sort of sense that she could have thought this was happening to her, for the assistant manager not to have stepped in before all this shit hit the fan, and for her not to have any worry or regard for the coworkers she supposedly "ditched" in the midst of a madman. Who knows?

This writer found something out while researching this quickly thrown-together book. While watching the part in the video where the branch manager is writing down the names of everyone on a business card, she mentions that the woman we know as the teller, with the initials EG, actually has a different job title. She's a Relationship Banker or (RB), as BofA people call it.

Who gives a shit? I do, and I will tell you why. The bank retired the word "teller" a couple of years ago while I was still there.

They now call it CSR or customer service representative. I always used to say the jobs there don't get better. The titles get longer, so you sound more important.

In 2020, when COVID closed down branches nationwide and totally not for the fact that banks felt like there were no sales to be had in the branch, I was told by someone who followed my socials about how they were "reimagining" the branches for 2021. Some of the stuff can easily be seen in the new branches opening in new markets. It looks like a fucking cell phone store with a couple of fancy offices strictly for home loans and Merril Edge investing. The teller window is pretty deemphasized in many new centers, often tucked away in the back, like this branch in Atlanta.

There are these newer branches called Advanced Centers, which are employee-less branches. There are a couple of ATMs and a couple of "offices" where you can video chat with an associate for those same investments and home loan needs. I am not one to poopoo remote work, as that is how I make an income these days, but why do you need to go to a weird empty bank to have that chat and not have it at home?

It's an illusion that the bank is in "your community to serve you," even though no one is there to help you. Near the end of my tenure there, I was taught at BofA to refer you to "the app" or the 1-800 number if you need assistance and not take ownership of something you may need. Using the app gives the bankers sales credit if they set it up for you. The 1-800 routed to a 3rd party call center in (insert college town name here) where someone who didn't go to college and is at their 8th call center job is trying to help you with complex bank issues with no real retail banking training.

James, you are going on a rant here. What's the matter? It is stuff like that I refer back to when you see something idiotic happen at the branch because it almost seems like banks revel in not having good customer service anymore. If BofA deemphasizes teller work, how can we expect the tellers to be "seasoned' as the branch manager put it?

This brings me back to the teller. Oh, I mean CSR. Oh, I mean Relationship Banker. Why does that title matter? Because as part of the "reimagining" of how the financial center works, the thought was there were no tellers anymore. The lowest job on the totem pole is Relationship Banker now, not teller. Even when I got it, that role was a sales role, not a teller role.

Here is my opinion on that job role.

Last year, Bank of America announced that the minimum wage for all employees would start at $25/hr, over $50k a year. I think the idea is if Bank of America is paying branch-level employees that much money, they will likely have to play an active role in the sales goal. With this pay raise, we can put this title on them, saddle them with a sales goal and sales training and focus even more on that while plopping their asses at the teller windows to "warm transfer" clients to an office to offer them a credit card or whatever.

I use the word "plopping" loosely because that assumes they are allowed to sit down at that branch. The 3 branches I was employed at never let me sit down as a teller. You should gander at my feet one of these days, and I'll show you the effects of that. Ha.

But if the "teller" was really a Relationship Banker, then that tells me she is more trained than the average teller starting out even a few years ago. You can't have her in that role, which I mentioned is a role with a sales goal, if she doesn't know shit. It's easy to call the teller stupid if you don't train her on these policy things and instead use that time to have her focus on sales only.

I would love to know if she was in an office most of the week, and the only reason she was out there in the teller window in the first place was that it was a busy Friday. It may not mean much to you, but it makes more sense to old bank nerds like me. Because in my opinion, you can't be faulted for something that a bank hasn't taught you. As immersive as the sales training is, I can only imagine how taxing it is to do teller training simultaneously.

Being an RB focuses you more on the sales element, which means you are adept at IDing the clients. Plus, you know that is more critical to that role when doing a service/sale request. ID guidelines are a part of every aspect of the "platform" side, as the bank calls it. Audits are performed to make sure you are in compliance.

This role used to be called sales and service specialist, which was the role I got in 2011. A decade ago, they wanted you to focus on non-teller stuff, which meant a more intimate knowledge of policy and procedure. I did almost 80% banker stuff, with only a small part-time role as a teller, mainly when it was busy, or someone was sick. I got to a point where I wanted to be off the teller window because it eats into the time I need to hit my sales goal, which if I don't hit it, I can be fired.

Her job title matters because it removes the "she's new" from the equation and leaves "she was poorly trained" as a more crucial factor. I mentioned already I wanted to know where the assistant manager, her direct supervisor, was in all of this before she sought him out? Again, if she was so new, the fact that he wasn't within a couple of steps of her was alarming as a former manager. You are letting the teller swim with no life preserver, which can create errors or a performance loss or cause something like this.

I always reference shows like _Bar Rescue_ and _Restaurant Impossible_ when making teamwork analogies because the hosts say it more eloquently than I ever can. If a waiter doesn't correctly and promptly enter his tickets, the cooks get slammed, shit gets forgotten on the plate or the wait time is long, and as a result, waiters don't get good tips, and everyone is pissed off. Suppose I were to take that she was "inexperienced" at face value. In that case, I assume that this is a poorly run branch as a trainee essentially was left alone to handle these challenging transactions without a net.

Jon Taffer would be in the grill of the assistant manager

right now. But to be fair, this woman is an adult, and you don't make it in this world as an adult unless you have common sense, which she didn't use here. I used to tell my teammates at BofA to make sure you don't cut corners when helping someone because you don't realize how much power your work wields on how clients go about their day, especially when there's an error by you. What more proof that a mistake by an associate can lead to bad than the cops putting a man in handcuffs? It was all because of your apathy and insubordination in not following protocol.

My Opinion: She should be terminated after her maternity leave. No way BofA fires her during the leave. They will wait. I think making a scene after she just has a kid isn't good business, in my opinion.

The reason for her termination will be not following protocol when escalating a dangerous situation which includes calling SOACC or triggering her silent alarm. Nothing with the transaction itself would trigger her termination, in my opinion, as the transaction was never completed and needed to be "approved" by a supervisor. I know it's crazy, but that extra layer of "research" is what they crave on high-risk transactions.

Lying to the police is not a popular move you can make and expect to keep your job. I have sympathy for the teller, as I am certain BofA training and a volatile work environment where branches are closed in her area, leading to interchangeable associates everywhere and a lack of consistency at work. I think that if she holds an RB title, that tells me that she's "more" than a teller and should have a little more seasoning than the bland-ass associate the branch manager made her out to be.

Playlist Viewing For This Chapter:

Video #1 (911 Call) In Full

Video #4 6:00-16:30

BLAME THE ASSISTANT MANAGER?

The most overlooked person responsible for everything is not the teller but the person in charge of tellers—the Assistant Manager.

In this book, I will not give the assistant manager's full name, though the manager in the police bodycam footage referred to him as "Mir." I have viewed his Linkedin page and can pretty much confirm that this is the man from the video. Many things on the Linkedin page make a lot of sense when you understand how this happened. But let's learn about the assistant manager.

Ahh, the assistant manager. Oh, wait, Bank of America changed the name of this job to FCOM, short for Financial Center Operations Manager. Again, it's another way for the bank to make its low-level people feel more important is to rebrand the job title. If you want to pick up a girl at the bar, you can lie and say you are a "branch manager." It's technically not wrong because your job is mainly to manage compliance, while the branch manager is more sales-focused.

Here's a quick funny story. When I was a 20-hour teller in Socorro, NM, they gave me business cards that had my name and location of my branch but no job title, so of course, when I was single and going to vacation destinations, I would lie to girls and say I was a branch manager. Don't worry. That's tame compared to the lying and deception you feel that you are part of at Bank of America, at least in my opinion

I despise the assistant manager role. It's a shit job, to be honest. I refused to apply for it 3 times in the last 3 years I worked there. My final branch manager, Barbie, straight up begged me to take the job after my bank fired Nancy, a great friend of mine, from the role to this day. I had never been asked to apply for a job in that way before. She was desperate because they were dropping like flies. If Bank of America was *Star Trek*, the assistant manager would be the guy in the red shirt that gets killed immediately.

That day that Nancy left in tears, Barbie said, "I don't want to give it to Stacie. It's yours if you want it." I didn't want it. I saw the stress of that job from the time I started at Bank of America. The branch manager, also known as FCM, gets all of the glory, 5 weeks of paid vacation, and none of the hard work in most centers. Before Barbie reads this and immediately gets that "What the FUCK!" look on her face that became my favorite, let me say that I never met a harder working branch manager in all my time at BofA. She got the job far too late in her career, and frankly, BofA underutilized her skills to the point where it's criminal.

She would likely say that most of the other branch managers are lazy asses, but I will let her speak for herself on that one. I never lost respect for her work ethic at any point in time. She got the job done and was the example I needed to work that much harder. Barbie did make me a better employee.

The FCOM job is the worst. It's the job most branch managers do before accepting a branch manager job. The FCOM has to train the tellers themselves, be their supervisor at the ready all the time, handle the "operations" of the bank, which includes gathering all documents and filing them for future audits. In recent years since Bank of America has mysteriously trimmed staff in branches over the years, they get bumped down to teller work. Yep, they cover lunches of the tellers, if the tellers even get lunches. You do everything and get paid $15,000-$20,000 less than the branch manager.

It should be noted some BofA branches have what is called "single manager financial centers" where this assistant manager role doesn't exist, and then it sucks even worse to be the manager. That's happening in a lot of smaller city BofAs.

My final assistant manager, Stacie, who was my friend for many years, took the job when I declined to apply for it, and Bank of America gave her the job with no pay increase from her job as a senior teller. I just remember her being pissed about that. They sold her on the title itself and not more pay. It is a fucking disgrace, and Stacie just grew to loathe the job until she walked away after they fired her other close coworkers and me. She hit the wall after 7 years of working hard with no reward.

In 11 years of working in Las Cruces, NM, I had nine assistant managers. Irene, Yvonne, Gloria, Joy, Kelli, Rebecca, Bianca, Nancy, and Stacie. At one point, I would consider the last seven assistant managers friends, and I got to know their families and saw their stress in the role. I never wanted that. I was an excellent little salesperson who hit his goal, and aside from the constant bullying by bosses with their words, they left me alone.

You needed to be a leader, and while I was that, I also knew the amount of shit that came with being in that role. The incident in Atlanta involving Ryan Coogler was a flashback to how that role is impossible to do. You get all of the blame for what goes wrong in your center. It's a no-win situation. You have to care about sales goals and teller metrics, and balancing. Twice the work with half the pay. Not cool. That doesn't excuse what happened to Coogler, though.

I think it's likely that if there is anyone who will be fired due to the Ryan Coogler incident, it will be the FCOM. Why? Let me tell you.

So, the FCOM is the "manager of the tellers." Bank of America used to have a teller supervisor role (TOS) independent of the assistant manager until they decided to add chores to the workload. Being the manager of the tellers also means you are responsible for their training. You aren't sitting there training them, but you are making sure their cheap headphones are hooked up to the computer in a break room so a webchat with tellers from all over the country can happen. The teller absorbing the training and being a good worker falls on you.

That must suck, considering the lack of being hands-on with training. Instead of learning policy and procedure, tellers spend an hour going around the board asking people what their favorite type of weather is. (I snuck into the room to see a few of these pieces of training over the years)

You are responsible for how good/bad they are even though you didn't have a hand in training them. When you get a teller out of that crappy training, you almost have to set up a teller drawer of your own and have them "really train" to learn how to do things. That's one reason service is terrible at that place. You have to do this while creating a schedule for the employees, making sure everyone is on their time, taking breaks when needed, and getting ready for the auditors who can come at any time.

Many people who have this role are also the vault tellers in the branch, which means setting up the tellers with money throughout the day and making sure tellers have enough available for large-dollar transactions like Ryan Coogler wanted. Yes, $12,000 is considered an insane amount of money to them. So the FCOM would have had an indirect hand in the Coogler transaction just based on getting the teller money to give to him.

The problem with the assistant manager in the Coogler story is that he was the most integral part of the transaction, whether you believe it or not. Bank of America tellers and former tellers alike would agree. Your tellers are only as good as your supervisor. If he didn't chat with the teller about how to escalate anything over her limit or what the "high-risk" transaction box means, then it is outright negligence.

Here were the assistant manager's roles in the transaction for Ryan Coogler. Number 1, just be present to be available for a limit override. Customer experience is something that BofA preaches about, so making sure a complicated transaction doesn't take an hour, he needs to be ready to be called upon for help. From the size of that bank, it sure seems like his only necessary focus should be on the ops side and teller side. It looks like a busy branch at all times.

Number 2, because it is a high-risk transaction, his other job aside from the override is to do research for the transaction. Some would say this is "extra work" because of Ryan Coogler's skin color. I assure you it's not. It is simply something that pops up that you can't get away from on the screen until you finish researching. In this scenario, you have to make sure the 2 IDs the teller had documented are valid and match what was saved on the system before. You also have to see if the transactions match his pattern, and in the case of Coogler, since he is a Californian in Georgia, can you spot some GA transactions in the history?

Plus, as part of the high-risk box, you can match his signature by looking at a digital copy of a signature card on file or look at the signature of any paper checks he may have written. It's a lot of shit you got to do. When all of that is good to go, the assistant manager has to put their bank id and password in to continue the transaction. Let's say it doesn't match, and they refuse to help them. They still have to enter their information to escape the transaction. That rule began right around the time I left.

This man is the King Shit when it comes to whether or not someone can get this amount done in the branch. I have seen instances where money is low in the vault, supervisors turn to using the high-risk box to turn people away to make up for not having enough in the vault for the rest of the day.

It's unethical as hell, but Bank of America has started cutting back on how much money it allows branches to order. Brian Moynihan said in an interview with Fox Business a couple of years back the "cost to ship money, move all this money around across the country was about $5 Billion", which to me makes sense as to why they cut back shipments for branches, ATMs, and ATM repairs when needed. It's basically going cashless by force.

Number 3, because of the amount mentioned in the previous chapter, he was likely the designee to make sure all CTR reports were entered into the system correctly. If the teller could get through that transaction without freaking out, he would have been needed at some point. Most branches have a designee to document all those CTR reports, and it would be likely that he was the one to do so. Long story short, he would have had ample time to confirm Ryan Coogler's identity during his original interaction to make a withdrawal itself or all the "paperwork" that had to be done afterwards.

This man holds a lot of responsibility, and I commend him for taking on that task. As I mentioned, it was something I never wanted. I would have instead gone straight to branch manager or market leader myself. But to have that job and the operations knowledge, or the "O" in FCOM, what they call the role now, you need to know everything about every position and task required to complete such transactions.

My experience is that 99% of people in the assistant manager's role were tellers at one point or another, so all the policy knowledge is learned before you get into management. He never had that role, so it makes sense how this could have happened.

Until you are left there with your junk in the wind waiting for help from your boss, you don't know how it feels. The customer thinks you are an idiot, and you are there just waiting to be rescued by your supervisor.

He doesn't understand the ramifications from the teller's perspective of the teller freestyling every step beyond the ones that require her to go to him for help. She should not be the one to deem Ryan Coogler suspicious and refuse to do business with him, and call the cops. That's the assistant manager's call because, as management, he has to defend the call made to have this happen, whether it was a legit robbery or not.

When you look at the branch manager's interview with the police on the bodycam footage, she clarifies that the teller went to her supervisor, the assistant manager, for assistance. The branch manager washes her hands of the whole thing with that statement.

She then mentions that the assistant manager went "into lockdown mode," which, if you believe the teller's angle, didn't happen because the assistant manager wanted to engage the customer to continue the transaction. The teller refused and ended up calling the cops. If you are an assistant manager, aka that woman's supervisor, and she goes behind your back like that, what example is that for other tellers? You've lost the room, in my opinion.

To be frank with you, I have never heard the phrase "lockdown mode" in all my years at the bank. It sounds made up, and it sounds like something you tell someone who is listening how finely tuned a machine you got there. It's simply not true. That phrasing isn't in any materials that train you for robbery or these incidents. Why exaggerate?

The assistant manager didn't do his job and let a subordinate dictate how this scenario played out and essentially called 911 and weaponized the police.

HIGH-RISK TRANSACTION

It sounds like a loosely run ship, and they got caught operationally with their pants down. I worked for 3 branch managers who ran tight ships, and trust me; this sounds so discombobulated. There should not have been a scenario where the assistant manager didn't even engage Coogler with eye contact and introduced himself as the person who would be helping the teller before the transaction started. Per the bank's training, it's just how things are supposed to be done.

On a busy Friday, he should be pitching in somehow to help the team. As an assistant manager, it is your responsibility to have an understanding that a significant transaction is coming before it causes a considerable delay for Coogler or the rest of the clients. What he should've done was he could have met Ryan Coogler at the door like I was trained to do. I hated doing it, but that was lobby leader training.

Barring that, he should have been hovering around his tellers, coaching them up and listening for clues that his engagement would be needed. It is not a sit on your ass job, and everything I saw from this incident made me think they weren't as into doing the job right as many would've been. The assistant manager did it the way he was trained at a previous job.

Social media has a way of branding these things on your brain forever. This incident will always float around the internet. We are always going to remember this branch, we will never not associate Ryan Coogler with this incident, and hopefully, you will remember this book with me tearing down a company that did this to him.

You have to throw a perfect game at life these days to get zero hate from everyone. Cancel culture is a scary thing for that reason. We are all humans who have flaws and make mistakes, but the mark of a real one is how you own those mistakes. Here, I can safely say that BofA, aside from a hollow apology, is not owning this mistake by taking action against the people who caused this poor man harm in Atlanta.

Social media and the internet allow me to understand who these people are. I have seen more on my TV screen streaming YouTube videos of bodycam footage than I have seen Chuck Rhoades on *Billions* and Rue on *Euphoria* this season.

The FCOM's horrible breach of procedure makes me cringe. I first noticed when you see the video of him debriefing the cops outside while they were rushing in. Based on his actions when the cops got there, it seemed like he was trying to justify the seriousness of the call. He tells the police outside, "He passed a note. Demanding $12,000. 'Be Discreet' and all that."

What's even worse a few seconds later in the same video, cutting off the police as they walk towards the teller line to let them know that he's going to go to the back (AND WALK IN THE LINE OF FIRE IF A ROBBERY REALLY WAS HAPPENING) to hand them the note, as if they needed it at that point before Coogler was in handcuffs. How the cops were not telling him to get the fuck out of the way was beyond me. In the photo you can see a person in the background. It's bAnK RoBbEr eXtRaOrDiNaRe Ryan Coogler.

HIGH-RISK TRANSACTION

But minutes earlier, according to the teller, he wanted to speak to the customer about the transactions. There are some fucking inconsistencies here, bro.

One other thing that I gathered from the video was that when he talked to the cops a second time before they went to interview the teller, he described the note to the cop at a teller window. What he says about the note and what this supposed criminal was trying to do was insanity.

In the video, he explains to the cop the note says, "Take $12,000 from my checking account. I want you to count it somewhere else, and I want this to be discreet." So, in a nutshell, this nutcase explains that the note describes what I see as a perfectly fucking normal-sounding transaction. Ah, nuts.

How did he not stop himself as he was telling the cop that? He should be describing it and then say, "Oh, shit. I think he was just telling us to take money out of his account and not be so damn loud. My bad." It's unbelievable he is telling that to a cop face-to-face and not saying "SIKE!" at the end of it. It's fucking unbelievable. Holy cow.

I learned about his background. He is still employed in the same role with Bank of America. That news may surprise a lot of you. It did me. But it has been quite a journey for Mir. Before accepting the role of FCOM at Bank of America, he was an assistant manager and "Financial Services Representative" at Suntrust in the same metro area. Suntrust isn't in my footprint here in NM, so I was unfamiliar with the super long job title. I looked it up, and basically, it is my old job, primarily sales.

Before Suntrust, he then had a sales role at Guaranty Bank/Best Bank, which has branches in Georgia as well, and then before that, he was the manager of Sunglass Carnival, which was an odd stop. Before being the manager of Ray-Bans, he had a role in Mastercard in India that may or may not have brought him to the US. He was an assistant manager there, but I'm unclear what he did.

All of this leads me to the beginning of this journey. On his Linkedin, his first job was with Bank of America! What? Weird! What's not strange was the job he had there, which explains a lot. His roles were Loan Counselor/Fraud Analyst/Team Developer/Assistant Manager. He was based out of India.

Now, there's one conversation I will not have with anyone, and that's the conversation about outsourcing. Every company does it, and honestly, many people won't like to hear this, but the quality of work is much better in a place like India for what his roles were. It sucks, but it's a fact. As I write this, the DOJ indicted ten Bank of America contracted call center employees in Arkansas for defrauding California unemployment [20] of over $2 Million, something I had predicted 18 months ago [21]. This shit would not have happened if Customer Service was in India.

The American Dream can include other folks from other

places. One of the few people I respected at Bank of America until the bank sold her branch from under her was my first branch manager. She was from Indonesia, and she ran the most efficient branch ever. I still marvel at how that small-town branch got things done. Because of my manager, international students who went to the university banked with us because they saw where she came from and the person she was.

That was a tradition I continued when I became somewhat important at my branch in this college town. I had international students, and they were a blast to talk with and see them prosper and get these great jobs everywhere. I will not fault someone for pursuing a unique journey like Mir, nor where he came from indicates work ethic. I bet he works harder than most of you.

Except that doesn't make what he did right. Here's the problem I had with this Ryan Coogler situation. As a fraud analyst, especially at Bank of America, the way you view things is skewed. At Bank of America, that role is done with beer goggles. Everything you see is a fraud based on what you are taught. From my excellent L-shaped desk here in Las Cruces, NM, that my fans on social media bought me, let me give you an example of what I mean.

I was a relationship manager in Las Cruces, about 20 miles from the Texas border. I ran into Texas customers from New Mexico and vice versa who had a weird issue: BofA would block their debit/credit cards for "irregular activity" because there were pending transactions in 2 states in a short period. I shit you not. I can only imagine people from NJ who commute into NYC having that problem. It would be millions of people.

There's a little town between Las Cruces and El Paso, TX, called Anthony. Half the city is in Texas, and the other half is in New Mexico. If you timed it right, you could use your debit card in two states in less than a minute. You can spit at a building in New Mexico that you'll use your card at while standing in Texas. Have I made my point enough?

Anyway, these fraud analysts would block cards without using logic because of the spirit of the reason for freezing the card. I would help clients call to get it unblocked. The analysts would say, "It'll be fine in 10 minutes". Often, that was BS, and the client had to wait until the next day to use their card. In some extreme circumstances, the card was closed, and a new card would be mailed in 7-10 days, and I would have to issue a temp card.

Fraud analysts, especially in a place like Hyderabad, India, where the IQs in the room lap mine like the way a Team Red Bull Formula 1 car would a scrubby F1 car at the Grand Prix of Monaco, are well-skilled at their jobs. However, the BofA school of logic gets in the way of the fraud department thriving, in my opinion. I was told that Formula 1 was currently an "it thing" again in the US, so I wanted to throw a reference in my book to that effect.

They are intelligent people, sharp as a bag of tacks, but the way fraud analysts learn lacks context as to why something may be irregular. The BofA fraud algorithms are shit, too, not catching genuine fraud when your chip is copied and someone 2000 miles away uses your card without a hitch. BofA pushes the app on you without the general public realizing that they allowed BofA to see their location, as most apps do, to be fair, to use that location when pinpointing irregular activity.

Identifying "fraud" by popping a giant red box on the teller screen already scares the shit out of the teller. You mix that with a jumpy teller and her supervisor who spent years learning horrible logic from BofA about how fraud happens and everything is a serious threat. You get a team ill-equipped to handle the situation any worse.

I had tons of clients with Indian heritage who became friends who are now engineers, doctors, and more. One former client is the Mayor of my birthplace of Socorro, NM. His son, Jeff Bhasker (22), a man who went to the same high school as me, is a Grammy-winning musician who produced Kanye West's last album. I can tell you that I am fascinated and proud of this assistant manager's career journey. But with all the praise comes the criticism that he couldn't have handled it worse. He is now tied with Ryan Coogler until the end of time for his bank's actions.

Knowing what he does now, I think he would have treated Ryan Coogler differently if he knew Coogler was a preferred client. He may have also learned about his celebrity, which would likely have changed the dynamic of the incident. The problem is, the assistant manager never got to the client. He assumed too much off of interaction with his teller. His training as a fraud analyst makes him think the worst of humanity immediately based on the shit those associates deal with in the fraud department. Talk to those risk management/fraud people with BofA who work out of Tampa, FL. They are the angriest people I have ever dealt with on the phone, and I have had bill collectors blow up my phone number for the last 20 years.

I wish him well, but I also wish he lost his job for this failure to perform his duties the way they should have been. His current Linkedin page has him at a financial center 30 miles from the incident. I won't name the town that's in, out of respect for his privacy, and also, I don't know if that's his actual branch, and he was borrowed at 1280 West Paces Ferry, where the Coogler incident happened.

If he got shipped there, though, that tells me one of two things. He's either on BofAs shit list, and they shipped him off to a suburban branch to wither and die on the vine. It's BofAs way of pushing the Vikings out to sea when they get too old and useless.

Or it could be they still think very highly of him. How can it be polar extremes, either excellent or terrible? Because when you succeed at the role, especially in a big city, BofA uses you to exemplify how good associates can be. Do they give you a comfy office for being so good? Fuck no, they send you across town.

I had a friend that worked at BofA in Phoenix for a decade.

I found her on MySpace (That's how old I am) on a BofA message board, and we talked shit about BofA and gave people pointers on how to do things better in our roles. Let's call her Lexi. When I first met her, she was a teller supervisor in Tempe. Then she kicked ass at her job, so they promoted her to Assistant Manager, but they shipped her ass to Avondale, which, if you know Phoenix traffic, that's a bitch to get there from Tempe.

When she killed it in Avondale, she decided to buy a house in Avondale with her hubby. Her boss said she would eventually be a branch manager in that general area within two years. That was until she got transferred to Mesa, a ridiculous commute from Avondale. Two hours in horrible traffic at times each way. When she asked to stay in that area, they pulled that whole "You should be grateful to have a job" shit with her, and she resigned on the spot and got a job at a BMO Harris Bank branch a few weeks later.

She was a star employee, and instead of being praised with a cushy role in her home area, they gave her a title and expected her to brave the AZ-202 every fucking day for peanuts. Great employees are rewarded with long commutes.

Last I heard, she's finishing law school. Guess that whole "You should be grateful" shit only works for people without options, eh?

My branch manager Barbie got transferred to El Paso Dyer St. as a "reward" for her excellent work, over an hour away from her home in Central Las Cruces. What a shit way to treat someone.

They eventually forced the branch manager at the only Las Cruces branch into retirement and installed Barbie there, but at the end of the day, they mistreated her as well. If anyone at BofA reads this (and I hope they will), she didn't tell me to say that. That's my personal opinion of what went down. P.S. You suck.

Anyway, this man knows banking, and he should continue his banking journey, but I feel that he should be punished for his role in this, which was marginalized during this incident because of how ridiculous the teller was. Good luck to you, Mir.

My opinion: Bank of America should terminate him for that lapse in control. When it punishes college sports teams for violations with academic fraud or recruiting violations, the NCAA cites "Lack of Institutional Control." That sounds apt for the assistant manager.

He let an ordinary situation that would take 5-10 minutes in a perfect world because of the forms needed for that amount turn into an hour-long ordeal where a man and his party in his car ended up in cuffs, accused of a federal offense for a seemingly ordinary transaction. He let the teller dictate how that transaction was going to go, and no matter the condition she was in, and no matter what she felt, he had an obligation to do his job the way he was trained to, and he didn't do that.

The frustrating thing for me is if she didn't want to help Ryan Coogler, the assistant manager theoretically could have had a cash drawer set up that day since it was a busy Friday. Then it would have even been more egregious because he could've quickly taken over the transaction at that point, but there was no way that he was the shot-caller here in calling the cops for this alleged "robbery," that's a problem. Like I said in the teller section, there were other associates, clients, and other people in the branch. If this was a dangerous situation, he didn't handle it well, and for that, he should still be fired because he potentially left those other people in harm's way.

FCOM/assistant manager/whatever BofA wants to call it these days is a tough job, as I mentioned, with twice the work for half the pay as a branch manager. Everything from every side of the bank has an element that falls into your responsibility. You are a trained dilettante, dabbling into different areas of the bank without genuinely focusing on the needs of one area. These days, post-COVID, the teller area needs more help because banks are busy, and branches choose not to hire as many people anymore.

The branch manager is more insulated from major discipline here, so this guy should be the biggest domino to fall. Sorry, dude.

Playlist Viewing For This Chapter:

Video #8 (Branch Manager Interview) In Full

Video #3 (Assistant Manager Debriefing Cops) 4:00-5:20

Video #2 (Assistant Manager Explaining Note) 8:15-9:00

BLAME THE BRANCH MANAGER?

The branch manager is the most interesting person in the whole situation here at Bank of America in Atlanta. I mean, talk about bad luck. My favorite movie is *Friday*. Although I don't partake in the movie's central premise, smoking marijuana, I love the movie nonetheless. I am immediately reminded of a scene where Smokey tells Craig, who just got fired from his job, and I am paraphrasing to clean it up a bit, "How the hell you gonna get fired on your day off?"

Although I don't believe she did enough to warrant getting fired, in my opinion, she almost could have on her day off. Why? Let's discuss this.

Why am I saying it's her "day off"? According to an interview with a police officer caught on his bodycam, she "just walked in" when it all went down. Whether she was on a very early lunch, was scheduled to go in at 10:30 on the first Friday of the month, or was being sent to that location for the day only, a bank manager would call all those options "A day off" because they know there are no actual days off at BofA.

Plus, the manager mentions that she's the financial center manager assigned to this branch today. Her name badge says "Dee" in the video. I will not disclose her last name because it wasn't on the video. I located her social media while researching this book. Thank goodness for the nametag. I researched her and others to understand who these people are and my feelings about them before going in deep with my opinions. I have a lot of issues with how they all acted, but I won't be a doxxer.

When I hear that a branch manager is walking into work at 10:30 on a Friday and she was a borrowed employee that day, I think this is likely an insane bank branch to be working at on a busy Friday. The branch manager just walking in either means the branch has no permanent manager because they either left the company, got fired, are on some kind of leave. What is likely possible in Atlanta is that the closure of dozens of locations, citing COVID as the reason to close them temporarily, finally are reopening back up and left a lot of spots unfilled. Managers are being passed around like the way Craig and Smokey pass the joint around in _Friday_. Damn, I got two _Friday_ references in one chapter about banking. Good work, James.

I was fortunate to have 3 branch managers in 13 years at Bank of America. I had long-term strong female leaders, and I fucking loved it. I didn't love a lot of my managers in the moment. Sometimes they made my life a living hell. Still, as I grew with the company and saw how their bosses treated them, I ultimately gained more respect for my managers because the regional and area leaders have their heads so far up their ass that you can taste their hair products. (I stole that line from an episode of _The Sopranos_.)

I also had a manager on medical leave for a few months before she ultimately retired. That was in 2014. I got to say the three months that we didn't have a manager was utter fucking chaos. We had an assistant manager, and she was more than competent to handle things, and we were adults who could professionally run a branch, but it was the little things. I didn't take one lunch break for 3 months. We had to take on a more significant share of paperwork, all of which had to be done every day, and we couldn't purposefully take on overtime. It was madness, and I hated it.

Occasionally, they would send a branch manager from another location. We only had one other branch in Las Cruces, so usually it was that lady, but a few times, they sent over managers from East El Paso, Texas, for 2-3 days. That is almost 100 miles away, and they couldn't give a shit less about our sales goals or operations being done. Their responsibility is their branch. If I did something wrong with a client, they couldn't reprimand me. They were just there. I distinctly remember two fill-in managers playing on their phones, one of which was audibly playing a slot machine game. I knew the sounds because my 70-something grandma played the same game I installed on her phone.

But you don't realize how much you miss them until they are gone. I can only imagine that if they were without a branch manager permanently on staff at that location, it was a total shit show over there even before Ryan Coogler walked into their world. There are a lot of issues with Bank of America in the Atlanta area from my perspective and my work doing my Notorious Banker project. The hours of video captured by police bodycams paints the picture of an inconsistent story that is trying to be assembled and then toppled over like a wobbly Jenga puzzle by the branch manager.

She walks into the branch literally around the same time the cops are there to arrest Ryan Coogler. I will get to the significance of this part later on. When something "of note" that is abnormal happens at your branch, you have to call BofA corporate security, and it is likely you are on the phone and emailing them shit the rest of the day. We had an older man slip on some ice once, and my boss was MIA all day.

I also had a man hit his knee in my office and ended up suing Bank of America off of that. When his knee injury happened, though, which was not a serious-looking injury, my manager had to fill out incident reports, police reports, and a bunch of other bullshit. I had to be deposed and interviewed by the bank's insurance company off of that incident. It was crappy.

Imagine the paperwork on arresting a man for trying to rob your branch and then finding out he was not a threat. She's probably STILL filling out paperwork if she is there. The crappy thing about being a temp manager is that you still have to answer for the people who are "under" you, even for the day. You didn't hire them. You don't even know anything about them, but you are supposed to praise them when they do good and "coach them" when they mess up.

The branch manager mentions to Coogler during a later "apology" that she "coached" the teller to Ryan Coogler, as if he has any fucking clue what that means. That sounds like a Bank of America manager, using all this bank jargon to show how professional she is. Trust me; I dealt with many managers like that in my day.

But I have to admit, at first glimpse of everything, I empathized with the branch manager at first because this doesn't seem like a mess a manager would get in. That is until I saw the first video with her in it when I downloaded all the cam footage. It was a six-minute conversation with a cop in what was her office for the day. She is seen talking with her market leader on the phone, who wants to know what's happening. In the video, she mentions how the teller "engaged her immediate supervisor," which is not how I would put it. Engaging him means "I need help," but she immediately said, "This weird man passed me a note." So that's not correct.

She mentions that she was told by who I assume was the

assistant manager that it was a "note-passing" situation. That was the first time I ever heard the phrase "note-passing" used the way she used it.

You would just say, "We think he is robbing the bank." I know it's the south, and unlike how different regions call Coca-Cola, a big Atlanta brand, "soda" and other regions call it "pop," I have never heard anyone in banking refer to this action the way they do. "It was communicated to him that it was a note-passing." It just doesn't sound right to me. I never heard a banker talk like that.

It just sounds like the assistant manager and the teller want to play up the note even when it is coming out of the mouth of the manager. She then says something even weirder. She mentions that he went into "lockdown mode." Again, this is another phrase I have never heard before, and I have taken the exact training they did. Lockdown mode sounds like something you set up on your kid's iPhone so they don't play Fortnite all day.

So, with the tellers still doing transactions for other customers, who are not scared or even aware of anything going on, Ryan Coogler is seemingly still chilling, waiting for his money, while the scared teller is hiding. Then, the assistant manager greets the police through an unlocked door. I figured you need locked doors for lockdown mode. He then walks with them and, with a normal voice, asks them if he should get the note for them, which would require him to walk down the same corridor alone where noted serial robber Ryan Coogler is standing during his reign of terror? Makes no sense.

I kid about the reign of terror thing. I am trying to chuckle through all this bullshit I have to write because of BofA.

The branch manager mentions that he followed their "certain protocols" at that point. I honestly cannot think of one thing he did right per protocol, but she seems to believe he did from what she knew. She then mentions the little secret about how they were stalling to buy the cops some time to get there. It's no little secret because, as I said before, if Ryan Coogler had done this for this amount before, he knows it would take a little bit of time to get done. It just would. Stalling occurs for standard transactions as well. It helps to break up the wait time in a client's mind.

She then mentions that she is putting a report together for "Monique," her protective services manager, also known as the person who likely put the smackdown on all their asses. She asks the cop if he wants to network with her, and he says no, because honestly, why would you want to continue with this? That bodycam footage is at noon, a full half-hour after the whole Ryan Coogler incident wrapped up.

That was the first video I saw, and I felt like she was trying to show him that she was, in fact, the person in charge and getting to the bottom of this, but I think she knows it's all a big mistake, but the bank won't let this end with the end of this incident that day. I am sure meetings are still going on two months later as I write this.

The other videos that recorded the events of the previous ninety minutes painted an even more inconsistent picture of how she tried to "handle" this. At 11:19 am, a police officer comes into her office and asks her for the teller's name because Ryan Coogler wanted it. This part is interesting because, as a former BofA employee, they pride themselves on privacy, up to and including with the associates.

Hell, I've heard BofA tell associates, including me, not to put photos of your family on your desk or in your office, "bEcAuSe SoMeOnE cAn KiDnAp tHeM." I write it like that because I always found it rather dubious that they didn't want to let you make your office comfier. They just wanted you to be an truly anonymous robot to your clientele.

But anyway, she fucking mentions the teller's name immediately after he asks, which weirds me out, because if there is a police report, and you know goddamn well there is, you hear the 911 call, and you have the cops interviewing her, they know the name already. The fact that the teller's name and assistant manager's name are written down so readily by her gives me vibes of "I want to throw these fuckers under the bus for doing this." Because any BofA associate would agree with me that the bank's corporate security would likely tell her not to give that information. It just seems like that would not be cool with them

The branch manager then mentions to the cop, "I intervened because she's pregnant and not 100%, and I am letting you know before communicating with her." It's weird because the manager and the teller were together about 20 minutes before that, while the teller was being interviewed by police. What?

It almost made me feel like she was trying to stuff the teller in a corner somewhere so that she couldn't say any more dumb shit, to be honest. If that isn't the manager's branch, and she and the teller never worked together before, it's interesting that she has such an intimate knowledge of her pregnancy and how it affects her.

If all the stress from the day's events made her not feel 100%, I could get that, but I don't understand why the branch manager is holding water for her here when she just gave her information out willy-nilly. She then mentions they are "all new to this location," which will lead me to a brief rant that I have been talking about since COVID started.

Let me just say it again. I will say it 10 times in this book, I'm sure. Bank of America has "temporarily closed" a lot of locations since the pandemic started, and I get why. I am not an idiot. I understand the need when things were terrible with case numbers and the uncertainty of COVID in the first few months of 2020. Nothing was open during the beginning months of COVID. But through all my googling, research of old news stories over the last two years, complaints I read and interact with on Twitter, among other things, I have concluded that a good chunk of branches closed were likely low-performing branches in regards to sales. Those branches tend to be in communities of color.

Now there is only so much googling of demographics and median income I can do sitting here on my desk, but I know why my branch closed down. My branch was in an area with poor Mexican folks and low sales growth. As a Mexican man who is currently poor, I will confirm this. As a former manager, the "richest' clients who visited my branch, per searching for that on Salesforce when making outbound calls mandated by BofA, are people who would be the lower-middle class in a wealthy state, which is not rich at all.

But when I discussed how Covid would close dozens of

branches in an area, the bank would keep one branch open and funnel all the clients there. It would be one big shit show to get anything done, and it seemed like they were only there to get any subsistence level of sales done at all when goals were paused due to Covid.

There was a relationship manager I interacted with for a couple of years in Philly. She was great and contributed financially to my project. Instead of a Philly cheesesteak sandwich, BofA served her a shit sandwich.

When COVID hit, she had her branch temporarily closed, and she was assigned to work from home. Her job was to test PPP loans after BofA gave employees a crash course on how they work so they can churn through applications (believe me, that part of COVID relief was a shit show that can be a book by itself). After several months of being temporarily closed and moving to work from home, she was informed that she would have to reapply for the job that she was at before the stay-at-home orders.

Here is what I believe. Part of the reasoning for pushing these employees to roles like testing PPP loans was to eliminate jobs at the end of this. How? The Philly girl told me that they had changed her job title, and she entered her time using a different "cost center" number, a defacto store number.

Why is this important? Because by changing the job titles and cost center numbers, those employees lost their "tenure." This practice is blatantly unfair. BofA has this rule about changing jobs no more than once a year. It makes it easy for BofA to let a lot of them go simply by saying the job is "ending," and that person is blocked from going back to their regular role.

So when you get old James to reapply for the job he had to leave because of COVID, and you say he has been shitty churning out PPP loans, you tell him, "You didn't get the position…oh, by the way, your remote work job was "temporary," and the role is ending." Boom, you let that person go without really "firing them." BofA employees become fucking Kohl's Christmas employees, where December 26th rolls around; boom, turn in your name tags and delete the Kohl's employees apps from your phone. You're done with us. Good job!

Why mention this? Because in Atlanta, there were some branches opened up only 2 days a week, plus some recently announced as permanently closing. I saw one bank closed on Wednesday for some reason, like it was some mom-and-pop restaurant, and you are curious why it was closed that day. Hours became bizarre at some locations across the country for no discernible reason (23) other than the bank blaming COVID. BofA's answer for everything stupid is COVID. COVID is technically a reason for this shit show that happened to poor Ryan Coogler.

A rag-tag bunch of BofA employees who don't know each other, don't know how to do things anymore after two years of COVID and are not communicating because they are thrown to a different branch every couple of days is a mess. There's no flow in the service, and you couple that with how a typical Friday is, and you are going to see some shit there. It's not the associate's fault that happened. It's not the branch manager's fault either.

The whole staff was so new that they didn't know how to interface with one another. After a decade-plus in the industry, I had moments like that myself. It's hard, and I can't imagine a new branch every day. Imagine having to switch high schools every day. That's not their fault. That's all BofA. BofA makes them shittier workers, not better, by doing that.

She mentions she doesn't have her business cards because her branch is closed down. See? That proves my point. I'm sure BofA is likely using COVID as the reason to make that decision for her branch, not the fact that certain areas bring in less money than, say... Buckhead. Buckhead is the wealthy part of Atlanta and the backdrop for the Ryan Coogler incident.

HIGH-RISK TRANSACTION

One note about her actions that day, and I will get to my opinion if she gets fired or not. At 11:32, she walked with the officer to the teller window to ensure they still didn't have Coogler's information there. Then the officer invites her over to the front door where Ryan Coogler is standing, and he kind of asks if she wants to go out there and say something, almost guiding her, as if he was her manager. Then at 11:23 am, on the police bodycam, she mentions something that sways me in the "they should fire her" direction. She says to the cop, "It was a misunderstanding. Is that where I am going with this? I had just walked through the door...."

It gets me so pissed. A whole hour of bullshit just happened where the cops and the bank concluded that, yes, it was a misunderstanding. She even said it was after all of this stuff, but when she goes to the door, she's unsure how to tailor that chat. It's like she is asking the cop for advice.

By the way, knowing how my old bosses were, she probably got dinged by her boss for wearing an old logo nametag that day to work. It appears clearly in the bodycam video. The red nametag went away a month after I left the bank in 2018. A new smaller tag with the new logo debuted in the fall of 2018, and protocol says to not wear them again. I bet her nametags are in the closed branch where she normally works. Yet, management would tell her, "It's no excuse, Dee." Ugh, I don't miss that.

In my eyes, that interaction where she is seeking guidance

from the cop is bad. To me, that's not manager material right there. I'm sorry. You have to own the mistake. Plus, the fact that she reiterated that she had just walked through the door as it happened just upsets me that much more. She had mentioned that. The cops, her staff, and her boss knew. Why is she trying to talk her innocence of all this into existence when no one is pressing her? Plus, here's why I get mad at this.

Go to 10:50 am, when the arrest of Ryan Coogler happens. Sure enough, the manager who said she "just walked through the door" was there, having just walked through the door. She sees a handcuffed Ryan Coogler getting led out of the bank. As the cops walk by with Coogler in hand, she whispers, "Good Job, Guys." What the actual fuck?

So, some people on social media, where I shared some of the police videos, said, "Maybe she is saying it to her team."

No.

Unless she was getting round-by-round updates as to what's going on there on the way to work, there is no possible way she knows what is happening with any potential robbery or incident like the teller claims was happening. Her reaction was for the cops rounding up a bad guy in "her financial center." Ryan Coogler could have been a homeless person taking a leak in the bank for all she knew, and the cops rounded him up, and she would've said, "Good job, Guys."

Her off-the-cuff compliment tells me that she was quick to judge and not a manager that asks, "Oh my goodness, what's going on here. My name is so and so, and I am the financial center manager. I just got in. What can I do to help?" No, she thought she was done with that bum in a hoodie being hauled off, and it was "Good job, guys."

She didn't do any research. She just saw a man get arrested and thought that was normal. It's just not normal. Seeing her commend the officers and then half an hour later, "Sincerely apologize on behalf of Bank of America" is the bipolar work environment I remember. We never did anything like that, though.

So when she finally meets Coogler, she hands him a card with all their names and info, and she mentions that she is going to have her market leader, Josh Roberts reach out to him. That sounds like it's all well and good, and he is getting a first-class ticket to talk to a real boss. Nah. Bank employees have to escalate to their manager even for stupid requests. Let's say a customer wants to be "on the record" about how awful the toilet paper is in their restroom, which inflamed their hemorrhoids. They have to document it like it was a severe issue. The gesture is meaningless. All they did was send it up the chain with a "commit complaint."

Josh Roberts likely sits there and makes these calls to "apologize" throughout the week. He will use his "empathetic language" and "enhanced listening" to speak to an angry client, promise them he will make a "note" of their issues, no pun intended, and make sure he has a conversation with the crew at the branch so that it never happens again. That's the whole fucking job. It makes you cringe to think they make six figures doing absolutely nothing for clients.

I used to be in charge of sending such complaints up the chain to our market leader. I hated that task. We were told to "find" 1-2 complaints in our center every day. I never got why. It seems like it could only hurt our performance reviews and by extension, our pay. Oh, so THAT'S why they did that!

The complaint escalation has very few teeth and is there to make the customers believe the wheels are turning for them. The market leaders care less than the people who document the complaints because all they give a shit about is new accounts.

She then mentions that the teller is "very new" and mentions the "coaching" thing I mentioned earlier in this chapter. Then that is when she makes her apology. She apologizes on her behalf and then says, "for who you are, a young black man, and two, for Bank of America." Ok. Now, of course, I think many people believe there is a racial element to this issue, and I believe there is too, and I will talk about it. The fact that she mentions to him that he is, in fact, "a young black man" is weird.

It almost makes the car that she is driving veer off a cliff. She made it about his race, which is odd that it never really got there during the whole chat with Coogler. The teller mentioned he was Black to the 911 dispatch, but that was only the context of answering her question. If Ryan Coogler was a young white man, would she have referenced his skin color? It was weird.

She then goes off on a "She (the teller) is with child (That's how they mentioned that Lucille Ball was pregnant in the 50s), she's "emotionally high," and "she's going through her own thing," whatever that means. I am going through my own thing writing about this shit at 1:37 am on a Friday after I had an emotional high from my New Mexico State Aggies winning an NCAA Tourney game.

She keeps on looking for excuses and then mentions that she "wasn't seasoned." Well, have Ryan Coogler bring the Old Bay next time he comes to the bank because the teller fucked up because she wasn't seasoned. So what's her supervisor's excuse? Is he not seasoned too?

She then mentioned how she just got there, and she wishes she could've been there to "assess the situation" and do more than just yell out, "good job, guys," to cops for arresting an innocent man. She then mentions Josh Roberts's name and how he wants to fake reach out again. The man runs all of West Atlanta, which tells you the size of BofA's market if there's a "big boss" just for West Atlanta. She goes to get her phone to give Coogler the manager's cell number. But before that...

OH YEAH, THE MONEY!!! He still needs the $12,000 he nearly could have lost his life over. She mentions she will take care of that, which is the most managerial thing she said, and that she will be back. Ironically, she will likely be using the teller's computer, who called the police to finish this transaction for him. That was the end of my videos with her in there.

I just want to say that all "platform" associates at Bank of America take training on how to listen to clients using "empathetic listening" or whatever it is called and are trained in how to apologize, or at the very least, acknowledge the client's concerns. While I don't doubt she is embarrassed about this and truly wants to apologize, BofA teaches employees how to "properly" apologize.

So, I debated long and hard whether or not to put her name on here. She has issues regarding what happened here, but it wasn't her fault. If she was assigned elsewhere that day and someone else was managing, it would've been them. We don't know how they would have responded, though. I decided not to after I found what I believe to be her LinkedIn (she's been at BofA the same amount of time that I would have been there) and her Facebook page.

After seeing what was public on her Facebook page and seeing that she is a woman of faith, which I respect, though I am not a person of faith myself. She is a graduate of an HBCU college, which I think is pretty special. She's a lady with a family and a smile on her page. I couldn't stoop low and make it personal about her.

One thing struck me on her page. She made a post last year,

which is very apropos to what happened here. I will only share the non-family part of it. She said, "Food for thought. In my line of business, I tell my teams you get the behaviors you tolerate!"

Damn, that's insightful. I mean it. I worked for the highest-rated and lowest-rated branches in my time at BofA. I know what she meant by this. The times we were terrible, we tolerated bad behaviors, it made our operations bad, and our sales sucked. The times we had great behaviors, we kicked ass. I like this a lot and will use it if I ever decide to manage a bank again.

BUT.... Here's a big but. Her team tolerated bad behaviors when it came to a policy decision. It cost a man his time, for a little while his freedom, and for a couple of weeks now, a bank's reputation, what little of it was not tattered. They failed her, and they failed their company.

I don't think she will be fired, and she is still there from the looks of Linkedin. I feel that her flaws as a financial center manager were exposed here, which was a problem. She didn't know how to come out and apologize to Ryan Coogler without getting reassurance from someone who is not a BofA teammate on what she should say. That was bad, in my opinion.

I believe she was just a victim of being assigned there on the wrong day, and nothing she did impacted how others treated Ryan Coogler. As she mentioned, that wasn't her branch, which means that it was only her team for the day and not a minute longer. I have no clue where her branch is, but I bet you it was closed "Because of COVID" by BofA.

My Opinion: I hate saying this, but I think she should go. The way I see it is that she had a valid excuse for not being there when it happened. When arriving, she praised the arrest before understanding what was going on. She was continuously holding water for the teller, making her seem like an invalid hot pregnant mess. She willy-nilly gives information on workers to a client when there are protocols that can be done to help him with that, even if it means a lawsuit is being filed. She keeps on trying to find a way to escape culpability in the chats with the cops and before talking to Coogler before she goes out and apologizes.

It's a fucking mess of a situation for someone not directly involved, but inevitably, in my opinion, I fear protocols were not properly done right. Period. I think away from the bank, she seems nice, but I can't see how BofA doesn't see her flaws on display in the police video.

Playlist Viewing For This Chapter:

Video #6 (First Manager Interview + Police Coaching +Manager Apology) 33:20-41:00

Video #8 (Branch Manager Interview) In Full

Video #2 (Branch Manager Praising Cops During Coogler Arrest) 7:00-7:15

BLAME THE POLICE?

      This chapter is challenging to write. My opinion may be complicated for some people, but I can tell you I am conflicted about talking about it too. Although I respect most police officers who have never done anything criminal or unethical, 2020 taught me that we should all be more vigilant of what's going on in our communities.

      In early 2020, before the pandemic and George Floyd, my little sleepy home county of Socorro county had a controversy on its hands. A police officer, who I know socially, was being outed on the local news for being offensive and racist towards Native Americans. He was arresting people and posting videos of the arrests with demeaning comments on TikTok (24). It was a fucking disgrace, and honestly, the fact that he still works for the city of Socorro is a travesty because there are a lot of Navajo folks in that area, and he's shown a particular bias towards them.

      So to tie my feelings on Bank of America to Coogler is easy.

HIGH-RISK TRANSACTION

With police? I am having a hard time pointing the finger so emphatically at what they did and calling it wrong. I know that may be a difficult pill to swallow for a lot of people. I am just trying to look at it from their perspective. These are the facts. They were going off of the information given to them by a dispatcher from 911 calls from the bank teller and possibly the assistant manager that painted a picture of an immediate emergency, a note had been passed, a robbery had been initiated, and people were possibly in danger.

We know that was wrong. I have seen a FIP arrest before in my region. It wasn't at my branch, but someone who was known to have been passing bad checks all over BofA in Texas was identified by a teller in El Paso as she was running the check. She got an alert on her screen that this was the defrauded account and to call the police immediately.

Because of the amount and the fact that it required an override, much like Ryan Coogler's incident, the criminal waited around because he thought the manager was doing what they usually do. Within 10 minutes, the police arrested him without incident. I remember the email chain from that day and how BofA preached that teamwork paid off.

Well, teamwork doesn't always win games. Sometimes people fuck up. The police officers quickly knew that someone aside from Ryan Coogler fucked up, and their tune changed within 15 minutes of the cuffs being on Ryan Coogler. They knew that all things being equal, they were just following procedure. I believe that for the cops. I don't think that for BofA.

They were "running a play," to use a sports analogy of how to handle this based on the scenario given to them. Don't you think they found it odd that the assistant manager walked up to them as they headed into the bank? Don't you think they found it strange that the assistant manager wanted to hand them the note that Ryan Coogler supposedly passed BEFORE they engaged Coogler to make the arrest? I don't think they are that stupid not to see the signs.

If I get a call of a robbery in progress, I walk in and have an assistant manager all on my balls about a note he wants to give me when a potentially crazed bank robber is in the lobby demanding money, yet the robber is standing there perfectly silent and still for minutes at a time? No way this is real life. I would immediately understand that some part of the tale is simply false. People are conducting business while this is all happening, making it weirder.

Yes, many people will mention that they had their guns at the ready. I am sure that is protocol AGAIN based on their information about a potential robbery in progress. There was no violent takedown. It was likely the easiest arrest they made all month, which should have also been a red flag for the cops.

So how can the cops be accountable for something wrong here? They weren't doing the bank's bidding necessarily. They were doing a civil servant's job to protect the community based on the info given. If I yelled, "This guy's got a gun," in a Walmart with a cop 5 feet from me, you don't think the cop instinctively puts his hand on his weapon? He would. Is that problematic or is it being ready?

I am no apologist for the cops. After George Floyd, Jacob Blake, a fatal chokehold that a Las Cruces (my hometown) city cop put on a suspect a couple of years ago [25], I am aware that this is a problem that needs to be addressed. How? I don't know. Police reform isn't my specialty, so anything I give you is just blowing smoke. I am not qualified to make that decision on how to combat this.

The way I see it is this. If you have in-laws, you'll get this. Do you have a great relationship with all of your in-laws, except maybe 1 or 2 that hate you? That family will define you as a person on the 1 or 2 bad relationships you have, rather than the 100 good ones. It's unfair, but it is the truth.

HIGH-RISK TRANSACTION

Most police officers love their job, want to help, and work hard. Some don't, period. It's like any other employee at any other job. Hey, it kind of sounds like bank workers! These cops in the Coogler case are thorough with how they pieced together the incident and figured out it was all bullshit pretty fast.

The most telling thing about the police bodycam footage is the times they are talking amongst themselves, and they just have this "What the hell just happened?" towards the end of the footage. The tone in their voice was like they can't believe this escalated to the level it did because of 1 or 2 lousy bank employees. That was the defining moment of the videos and mainly one of the reasons I wanted to write about it, because those cops don't understand bank policy, yet they know what they were told doesn't match up with what they were seeing.

If I had to find fault in the performance of the Atlanta PD in this incident, it is simple. They were too nice to the teller and manager in charge when asking questions about what happened once they deduced that it was likely not a violent situation. Once the fact that this was not a robbery was snuffed out, not everyone got to go home and eat ice cream. Some questions had to be asked about the misuse of 911, omission of facts when calling 911, and the lack of following protocol, including deciding that there was a robbery happening here.

The manager's preamble about not wanting the teller to be grilled because the teller was pregnant and in an "emotionally high" state would not fly if a robbery actually happened. They need to document all this shit immediately. Because there was no imminent threat, why did the cops give her a pass? Was it more like a "You fucked up royally, you will get in trouble at work, and you are likely embarrassed beyond belief. Punishment enough for you."

I don't find fault in them writing their names and badge numbers for Ryan Coogler. While I don't know the point of asking for that info, I understand why he would want it. The police knew that policy and protocol was followed and that they weren't at risk of losing their job, unlike the BofA folks. That is why they gladly gave it to Coogler. In the videos released, they are pretty fucking pissy about it, though.

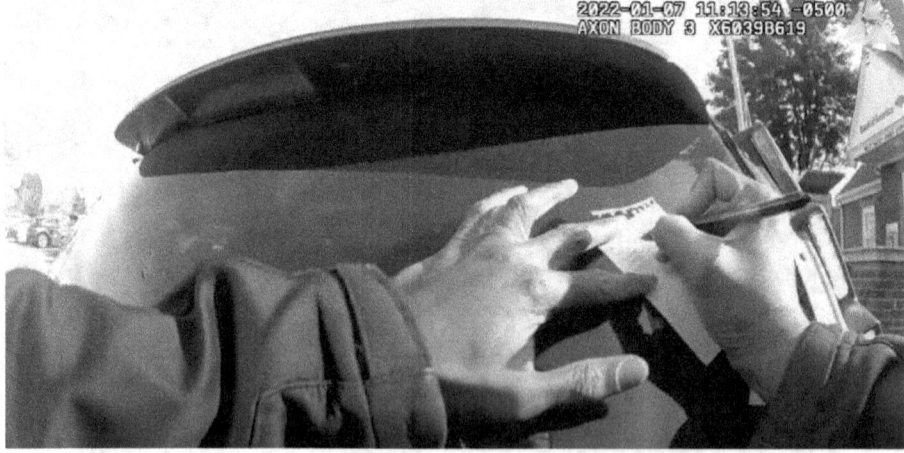

I find fault in the officer coaching the bank manager on what she should do/say before apologizing to Ryan Coogler towards the end of all the videos. It's not their place to repair this relationship. When tensions are running hot, and the cops said that Coogler was a different level of mad, then you need to say, "You know what? Let's not have this chat today!"

I fucking find fault in how the cops give unsolicited bank advice on how Coogler should go about doing this transaction in the future, so this shouldn't happen. They don't know that bank. They don't know the protocols of an electronic withdrawal. In my professional opinion, they are trying to find fault in something he did, which is angering because there is nothing he did wrong.

The thing I loathed the most was when the cops were berating the people in the car, being smart asses to them, when the arrest was first happening. You feel the unnecessary tension spewing from the cop who is yelling at them for no reason other than they seem far too casual and loosy-goosy with him. That's probably because they aren't fucking accomplices in robbing the bank!

I know BofA wants to get in front of this and say, "I'm sorry," but the cop is leading the branch manager, whose sincere apology is questioned by me, to a heated guy that her staff called the cops on a few minutes before. That part was just weird.

After the George Floyd incident, there were a couple of horrible incidents in Atlanta. During the protests immediately after the Floyd incident, the APD was caught on tape extracting two Black college students from a car during the night of one of the protests and tasing them (26). Six cops were charged, four were fired, and two were later rehired after that incident, which angered many people, including former mayor Keisha Lance Bottoms. Seeing the video of that was horrifying. Go to Youtube and search Messiah Young and Taniyah Pilgrim, and you will see what I mean.(27)

Then the **killing of Rayshard Brooks outside of a Wendy's in Atlanta** (28) at 125 University Ave SW, 10 miles from the BofA branch in question. Officer Garrett Rolfe shoots and kills Brooks, who was asleep at the wheel at Wendy's drive-through, blocking traffic. He then pulls him aside, performs field-sobriety tests, and after a frightened Brooks took the cops' taser and ran, Rolfe killed him in the parking lot of Wendy's, where people were still getting their late-night snacks. More unrest happened, the **Wendy's ended up being set on fire** (29) and there are some weird legal filings where the **cop arrested for unjustly killing him is getting back pay.** (30)

It is all a fucking mess.

So I can understand how the African-American community feels about Atlanta PD, and I get how this feels like another strike. But think of it this way. Does the criminal activity of those cops I mentioned mean that speeding tickets and reckless driving arrests should stop? Does this mean DWI Checkpoints need to go away? No. Police work is necessary, and along with every job, maybe some more training is in order. Fuck "maybe." Everyone should have extra training.

But they did nothing wrong (or I guess I should say excessive) here. I sincerely believe that. There's nothing I feel needs to be answered aside from the lazy questioning of the teller when she was the linchpin of all this shit happening. She got let off the hook by the cops in the video. Plus, I guess I can fault them on the one officer's guidance on how the manager should apologize, and the unsolicited advice to Ryan Coogler on how he should bank was a bad look.

My opinion: Nothing happens to the police officers in this incident. I feel that a legal settlement with the city might have occurred, and we were in the dark. I think that the City of Atlanta, mainly since the aforementioned violent incidents where they had cops arrested, is still fresh in the minds of many, that they investigated and found that protocol was put in place under the circumstances they were given. To shade the cops here isn't right only because they can only respond to what they know and are told at the moment, not what we find out afterwards. Simple as that.

Police officers need constant refreshers on training like any other job out there, but based on the nature of the call, what they knew, or didn't know, and how the bank was treating this, they were manipulated by the bank here pure and simple.

Playlist Viewing For This Chapter:

Video #2 (Arresting Coogler + Interaction with Manager and Asst. Mgr) 6:00-9:45

Video #6 (Cops Detained Coogler's Party While Other Cops Are Detaining Coogler) 4:00-12:00

Video #2 (Cops Complaining About Coogler Asking For Their Badge Number) 25:30-End

Video #7 (Cops Discussing What The Bank Went Wrong) 4:30-9:00

Video #4 (Cops Discussing Coogler's Transaction As Legitmate) 15:30-16:50

Video #6 (Cops Talking About Case Amongst Themselves) 40:40-44:40

BLAME RYAN COOGLER? (HELL NO!)

I wanted to note that I will NOT be including direct photos of Ryan Coogler in this book. It's a personal decision. I feel that the incident we are here to talk about is a lot for the poor guy to have to deal with already. I think including a direct photo of him in this is unfair to him, regardless if it's on the police video. I can't control what is on the video, but I can control what goes in my project. He's a stronger man that I can ever be after something like that.

Let me start this very brief chapter by answering what I think is the correct answer to this question. 1 Answer = $1,000 of the money Ryan Coogler was requesting. Ok. Here goes. No. No. No. No. No. No. No. No. No. No. No. No. 12 "No" Answers = $12,000 or the amount he wanted to take out. Ryan Coogler did nothing wrong. According to this former Bank of America manager, there was evidence of him being trained on how he could make the transaction smoother.

First off, he used the QST (the machine you put your debit card in), entered his PIN, and presented his California ID. That sounds like a person walking the lobby in some bank (the lobby leader) he's been in before taught him to have all that shit ready. With some customers, it's a struggle to let them know what they need for that, but he was on it. Ryan Coogler was prepared.

Secondly, the note that he wrote, which we have been over and over on, was written in a way that, of course, looked like this hadn't been his first rodeo. He knows how loud the money counter and the piece (hand) counting can be. He knows he doesn't want his name used out loud for fear of attracting attention. He knows more about the steps than they did.

Thirdly, he was not perplexed at the length of time it was taking to help him when they were busy calling 911 because he knew that it was a process. It's possible that he's been in some crazy long lines with long wait times, so he kind of knows what to expect when going into the bank. The managers and even the police officers mentioned on the bodycam footage that having someone go up to him and ask him if he has been helped is part of the process of stalling while they call the Federales. Unequivocally that is bullshit. It's not even remotely true.

It's the bank's version of mixing metaphors. Yes, they do that stall thing when researching a transaction to be FIP (Fraud in Progress). It usually involves a fake check or a stolen identity. There was none of that here. It was a man with a card, an ID, and a directive to HIS account number. If the note-passing was what they think he was, then by all accounts, he is a bank robber, or at least an attempted one, correct?

If this stalling thing was the procedure, sending people directly up to an alleged "scary" bank robber with your fake cheeriness and willingness to help is a fucking violation of all those employees' rights. No bank I know would have fed an employee to the lions in the colosseum to give them time for the cops to arrest him. What fucking sense does that make?

Because seeing how we verified things and made people wait at my branch, you do the checking up on the customer to break up the time, to make it seem like less time is being spent than it is. I vividly remember one case that happened to me. A customer of mine was a county judge, and much like the Paul McCartney song, "Band on the Run," he sure as shit held a grudge against us after one bad day.

One slow day, a guy with many tattoos came in with a $6,000 check from the judge, and it said on the note of the check, "Camaro." Knowing the old man judge as we did, we didn't necessarily THINK he was into sports cars, much less interacting with this big, tough guy, which was the bank branch's mistake, and by extension, mine and my boss's screw up. She didn't want to cash it because of the amount and because it was check 1002 in the judge's checkbook, which red flags it immediately as possible fraud because most people start their checks at 1001.

So naturally, the guy stole a book of checks and wrote one to himself for a fake Camaro, right? That's what BofA wanted us to think and believe through training. So my manager told the guy, who we were trying to pin as a crook, that we needed time to "verify characteristics," whatever that means. I was tasked to call the judge. I had a cell phone number on file, which I called, and he didn't answer because.... You know, he's a judge and stuff and his hours are bank hours. I left a voicemail. I was then directed to call his house because we know judges are at home during the open hours of the courtroom. No answer; I leave a voicemail.

My boss tells me to call his cell a second time. No answer. I was then told to flat out refuse the check because "We can't independently verify that he wrote the check." We had no signature to match it with and no history of check writing. I go to the guy with that story, and immediately he thinks that he got scammed out of his Camaro based on how I needed to word it per policy.

He fucking freaks out and sends a bunch of texts and calls incessantly to the judge's cell phone himself. I told the guy there was nothing I could do for him, and I called the next person into my office. Five minutes into that chat, my internal direct line rings incessantly, and I see it's the judge. Shit. I can't answer it. He calls about ten straight times to my direct line, but I am stuck with a client. When I finally finish with that client, I call the judge's cell back, and he's fucking furious, "It's my money. Who are you to fucking say how I spend it?"

I'm pale as a ghost on the phone as he just wails on the bank and me for refusing to help this guy. The judge asked why I couldn't have texted him (We weren't allowed to on our personal devices) because he was in session and had to take a recess because the seller of the Camaro was bugging him with texts and calls after we refused him. That judge sent a letter to my direct boss, who then COMMENDED our branch on being cautious with our clients. Yeah, but we alienated a longtime customer.

The reason I tell this story is that if I called the judge, he answered and said he didn't write the check, I would then have to follow protocols to call the cops on this guy, and that would easily have taken 15-20 mins more on top of the 40 minutes I wasted. It's a pipe dream to think that crooks will just stand there waiting to be taken down by cops. If Camaro guy were a crook and knew we were onto him, he would bail in two seconds. But he didn't. Why? The Camaro was real.

Ryan Coogler saw nothing wrong with the transaction presented. Think about it this way based on his job. Directors are always finding the best ways to tell a story through pictures. This instructional note on a deposit slip was his "method" to use a Hollywood term to get his point across to an audience of one. The note was to make that connection to the crazy teller.

How is "please be discreet" on the note any different to people who order on mobile food apps and direct how their food is prepared, cut, don't let it touch other foods, sauce on the side, etc.? It's unorthodox, but they adjust to your individual transaction. At least they should.

Why is the bank the one place he can't use that way to get the point across? Don't say because it was a note, ok? Please re-read that part of the book. In his eyes, he was helping the teller more than anything by cutting out all the small talk and giving direct instruction. Eighty percent of being a teller is asking questions. He answered them for you. What's the problem?

I have seen people find fault in his choice of sunglasses, a beanie, and a hoodie. It was fucking cold that day! You don't take off the beanie when you go into the bank, just like if someone was rocking a 20-year-old #40 Sterling Marlin NASCAR cap, you likely wouldn't ask that man to take his hat off.

My dad wears baseball caps to the bank and everywhere, for that matter. My father-in-law wears hats to the bank. He may even wear a bandana if he's on his bike. He's a 50-something man. Yeah, he can likely kick your ass, but he's no more a threat to you based on his clothes, so why is Ryan a threat?.

Do you ask someone wearing a parka to take it off when going into the bank? No. A parka isn't a weapon, but you can carry a gun inside a parka. Get one of those North Face ones, and you can have multiple guns and bombs. Fuck the note. (I'm kidding, calm down.)

When we nitpick shit like this, it impacts us all because we are participating in a game that can also likely find us in trouble down the road because if we aren't all uniform in the same clothes, same demeanor, same monotonous lockstep in a line like some wintertime Moscow bread line from the USSR days. We must be a suspect anytime we freestyle for ourselves instead of what these unwritten rules say we can do, right?

People are ragging on him for a mask as well. (Sigh) Aside from the COVID shit, I mentioned here and in a more comprehensive BofA/Wells Fargo book I am writing, I don't want to talk about mask-wearing. It was so last year. I still wear a mask to the gym even though mask mandates say I don't need to. Why? Because the only time I seem to get a cold or the flu, a hardcore gym session precedes it. No one sprays down machines, it's stuffy and gross at times, and it doesn't feel spotless even when gym employees try to keep it clean.

If I could wear a full-body condom to the gym, I would. Ryan Coogler was not a threat because of the mask. Blame BofA for that. It was required to go in. Every customer they have helped for two years has worn a mask. They still have mask mandates at their locations as of January 2022, the last time I cared to look, and the month this happened. I know this because of the crazy anti-mask, anti-vaxxers bitching about it in my Twitter feed when I search for Bank of America stories.

My wife and I watch *Chopped*, and the one thing I always like is when someone makes a perfect dish that all the judges loved, but to keep the suspense for good TV, someone will find something to shit on, even though they don't mean it. It usually sounds like this. "Well, if I had to find one thing to pick on, it's the plates you used, and I would have maybe julienne the carrots instead of dicing them."

Things that don't matter to anyone, but they have to nitpick for TV because that's the show's premise. If there were one thing where maybe something happened that only enhanced the police officers' belief that it was something more would have to be his party in the car. The two people waiting for him in the car, with the car running, are why I think the cops amped it up a little bit. That's not my nitpick or criticism, but merely me saying if you can find one abnormal thing in everything as a whole, I would say that would be it for the police officers.

Yes, I know it was cold, and you want to leave the heater on for the people in the car. Yes, I know they didn't want to get down with him. Some people have phobias of banks, believe it or not. But you couple the call with that sight, and I think it only pushed the cops into thinking that they had a significant situation.

In the 911 call, It's conveyed that Ryan Coogler was acting strange and weird with his actions from the teller's POV. Is being weird a crime? Is looking weird a crime? If so, lock me up. I'm the epitome of weirdness, and I am sometimes standoffish to people. That doesn't mean I will rob you, nor does it mean I warrant any special attention. He didn't deserve any special attention for anything he did wrong that day. Frankly, it's "weird" of you to think he did.

Ryan Coogler deserved better, and the fact he is making 99.999% less of a big deal about this than me says a lot about the man he is. What happened to him was a horrific incident, and there's no reason I would fault him for protesting on these assholes every day if he wanted to. I hate it for him that Banking While Black will now be synonymous with his name.

To have many people on social media just to look for something to blame him for during this incident tells me we just have people looking for a reason to shade someone for any number of reasons. It sucks that just because he is an African-American guy, he has to hear this negative shit from people about he somehow did wrong during this. It's the fucked up part of this because who wants to side with the bank of all things? Give me a break.

He is a victim of bank policy, profiling, and a bank trained to rid themselves of risk by just being the worst to their clients. If Ryan Coogler reads this book, I hope these thoughts find him well. As a former sweet-talk trained associate for that company, the apology that BofA gave had all the sincerity of a birthday greeting on Facebook.

DID RACISM HAVE A ROLE DURING THIS INCIDENT?

Yes.

[End of chapter]

DID RACISM HAVE A ROLE IN THIS INCIDENT? (MORE CONTEXT)

Yes.

Oh, wait, you want more? Ok, I guess.

I know it's not proper trying to be funny here, but a 3-letter word is all I need to convey that yes, in my opinion, I believe that Ryan Coogler was the victim of racism here in Atlanta, GA at Bank of America, though not as direct as you would think. I think it goes beyond, "Black Man goes into the bank, is mistaken for a bank robber because of all the scary vibes he puts out." That's the easiest path to get where you want to go, but this isn't Ferris Bueller cutting through his neighbors' yards to beat his parents and sister home.

Is that a dated enough reference? Sorry. But here's the thing. Half of the followers of my project, The Notorious Banker, are people of color. I think it is because they understand what I am discussing. Being a person of color myself, I can state that what people perceive as poor service is racism cooked in a stockpot with piss poor training and lousy policy, which leads to all these issues at banks.

Let's forget about Coogler directly, and let me take you to a couple of other stops which lead me to this conclusion.

Ever go on Youtube and search "Banking While Black [31]"? Do it one of these days. You will see a couple of examples that happened to others in the last couple of years that made me more prominent on social media as I charted my path to doing my consumer advocacy project to help people burned by big banks.

You will see Ron Escobar's video. [32] He's a business owner in Southern California with 12 employees. He issued payroll checks from his business checking account at Bank of America on a typical Friday. They all went to the same branch to cash the check, which resulted in an $8 fee to cash the check if you aren't an account holder. They will ask you if you want to open an account, but that is no requirement to cash the check. Anyway, they cash the checks of 11 of the 12 people, all of them not Black like the 12th one. The 12th one is told he can't cash the check there; no reasons are given.

Now, it pains me to say it, but because this happened to Coogler as well, even though he is a client of BofA, this rings all too familiar to me. We were taught at Bank of America to send clients to the "platform" side (the people in offices) to have their checks "verified" by bankers in order to cash them.

Regional managers found this a strategic way to do something unethical. It was not necessarily discriminating against people of color but enhancing sales by getting the trained talkers involved in a banal transaction like cashing a check and pushing those folks into becoming clients. They will let the customer simmer in the lobby, invite them to the offices where bankers are, try to sales pitch them on an account, and if they say yes to you after all that hoopla, excellent. We got a new customer.

They typically let the customer cash the check with the tellers if they say no to the sales pitch. But the procedure of leaving them waiting is to get the client to say, "Fuck this. I'm not coming here again. They take too long to get me my money!" That's what BofA wants. If you will never be a client, we don't want you to make our line longer for the clients who make them money.

You may say, "Well, ok, James. I understand that. But why is it racist?" Because you will realize that in many areas of this country, the folks who come to the bank to cash checks that don't hold accounts are people of color more often than not. When you are doing this bullshit to either force them to bank with you or drain them of one thing they can't get back, which is their time, it is discriminatory.

After likely going 0-11 with cashing checks for Ron Escobar's employees, they presumably were pissed that they couldn't convert those into new customers, so they were not thrilled about doing it a 12th time. Another element is some market leaders, including my former leader, would make us report how many nonclients we had cashing checks and how many teller warm transfers we had close into new accounts. This was done via midday conference call. We had to lock ourselves in our office, not help clients, and speak to why we can't sell sell sell. The number was never good enough for them, and we got chewed out every fucking Friday.

Do I think the 12th guy got denied because he was Black? Partly. I also think many people in banking think they are smarter than their clients. I probably foolishly thought that as well at one point in time. Delusions of grandeur, even when you are replaceable cog in a billion-dollar bank. You see a guy who happens to be Black, and it's the same spiel to try to get them from going to the branch. You think it is unlikely the person will make a stink about what you did, right? He's had worse said to him because he is a Black man, right?

Bullshit. Here is a movie analogy for you. Think of the movie *The Waterboy*. In the bowl game, Adam Sandler's team is going to kick off, and the kicker wants to kick an onside kick to retain possession. (33) He will kick it in the direction of someone who doesn't appear ready for the ball to be kicked at him. He pans through all the players until he sees one guy shaking in his shoulder pads. He chuckles and says, "Oh yeah. There's my bitch."

While a crude way to analogize, I think that bankers tailor how they treat people by appearance. How can you say that's not possible? I had a reputation for being a flirt, and frankly, any of my coworkers who became family to me will laugh and chuckle about how I lit up around women. It felt like I worked harder and better around the fairer sex. My work ethic changed depending if I helped an attractive woman or not.

HIGH-RISK TRANSACTION

The fact that I didn't have that same level of service when I had men sit down with me made me technically discriminatory. While not as egregious as picking the Black construction worker to play hardball with at the bank, it's still wrong. I apologized many times for how I could be when I wasn't focused on just work. It's crazy to get older and see the flaws of your youth. I want to own them simply because I want to make sure service gets better at these places.

So his African-American employee is unable to cash a check. This business owner does something that I never see in most business people. He sticks up for his guy and drives to that Bank of America branch and seeks out the person who is fucking over his employee. While waiting to speak to the manager, he and the employee are chilling, making small talk, and he mentions how they had a little satisfaction in telling him "no," and he said they said to him that "he would have to go through this every time he came in." "This" means waiting around while they "verify" the check to approve it to be cashed. This shit wastes your time and acts as a deterrent for going in.

The business owner, the fucking apple of BofA's eyes because of how much those clients can get you for your sales bonuses by upselling them on a suite of products, has to wait 15 minutes to speak to a manager about why they wouldn't cash his employees check. When the manager comes up, he sees Escobar recording, and he refuses to talk with him anymore because he is recording. Now, of course, recording on private property is a no-no, but at the same time, the banker is holding onto that rule like his balls to get out of explaining the very unexplainable situation that they created.

Escobar then agrees to turn the camera off, but the manager still refuses to meet with him, which pisses Escobar off more. After waiting for the cops to get there, the manager finally decided to help Ron Escobar and explained that "the writing and signature didn't match his previous checks" and "they don't call to verify checks." The second part is true, depending on how stupid your region is. Still, the African-American employee's check was written the same day as the others, so they couldn't POSSIBLY have been able to cross-check signatures against checks written that day, at least not on the system.

What is possible that could have happened from the bank side is that there could have been an "out of sequence alert," which occurs when a business writes a ton of checks, and they cashed out of order. For example, when check 999 gets cashed before check 400, and then check 1000 gets cashed after that. It happens. I had an Arby's franchisee cause us those issues before. But a good bank would have known that happens and still cashed it anyway after careful review.

It's maddening watching that video because I know the manager is lying. He's trying to protect his associate, and he doesn't have the skills nor the desire to try to fix it. I can get where he's coming from, not wanting to deal with it. He's a low-paid, overworked assistant manager, so I get his hesitancy to get in the weeds here. The assistant manager's name is Christopher B. Gomez, and according to some research I did, he no longer works for the company.

I don't blame him. How the fuck can you escape that mess you created at your branch. When I googled his name, a person came up who looks like him and is an actor with an IMDB page. (34) His most notable role is "Concerned Onlooker" in a movie short called "Do You Know CPR?" and an uncredited role in a Batman sequel a decade ago. If that is, in fact, him, congratulate him for getting out of a bank where he had to decide which customer to help and which to screw over.

This video has been shared millions of times on social, and what can I say? It's essential to have this on social media because an incident like that happens often. The Ryan Coogler incident just brought this issue of branch discrimination to prominence. It's just when it goes viral with someone we hear about it. Others,

HIGH-RISK TRANSACTION

for years, have just sat around and taken this shit from banks. It has to stop.

A month before Ryan Coogler, I got wind of an Instagram live stream from the rapper Boosie Badazz. (35) He was at a Bank of America in the Cleveland, OH suburbs, where he was trying to negotiate a cashier's check for $6500 that his business manager had just printed out for him earlier that day at the exact location.

Business managers for celebrities will typically do things to keep accurate spending records. I dabbled in the music industry as a writer before I got into banking, so I am familiar with how bands use their money. When Boosie went to the bank to cash the check, despite having an ID and debit card like Ryan Coogler did, the bank manager refused to cash the check, likely because of a prompt on the screen that comes up when a cashier's check is printed and attempted to be negotiated the same day.

Of course, BofA thinking they are the most intelligent people in the room, just flat out refuse to help him negotiate it. Boosie claims he has $2 Million in the 9 accounts with them and even asks if a call to his private banking manager would help speed this up. She ignores that request.

While in the live stream, the woman seems more helpful than in the Escobar case. She makes it sound like the system just refuses to let her do this transaction. In reality, verifying someone on the system, using your bank ID and authority to override the system can come back on you for making too many exceptions, and she didn't want to waste that on HIM because it can be done.

Despite BofA being new to the Cleveland area's footprint, they are still fucking trained managers, right? So she then suggests to him that he should deposit the check, and take an equal amount of cash out, which makes no sense. More transactions, more work, and honestly, since Boosie is in the Boosie BUSINESS, his statements look fucked now because a bank manager refused to help a million-dollar client with a simple request, a $6500 check cashing. It's something that an accountant will ask Boosie, "Why the hell is this weird multiple-step transaction here on your statement?"

He leaves the bank talking about how he will leave them a bad review, which is good because it can impact their quarterly payout, but the problem still arises that a woman didn't feel comfortable because a Black man wanted a large sum of money.

You can see in the car how emotional and pissed he is while he is talking about it. He doxxes her, which got me a 12-hour suspension on Twitter for sharing his video. I am OK with it. You can tell it hit him the wrong way, and Twitter and Tiktok blew up. I got over 3 million views breaking down what the teller and manager did wrong.

I reached out to Boosie's management team and told them how he should handle this incident, and I got thousands more people to my social channels to explain this incident and others with context.

I will say I did get a lot of angry emails from people who disliked Boosie for his comments on basketball legend Dwyane Wade's child, who is transgender. I find the comments abhorrent, but hear me out on this. That doesn't excuse how he was treated at Bank of America. If these 3 high-profile videos don't convince you, how else can I do it? Well, let me try to help with that.

I, for one, have always thought, especially in my most recent bank role at Bank of America, that the requirements to avoid a monthly maintenance fee have elements of racism or classism to them. I know some may think I am crazy, but hear me out. BofA's primary checking account (36) requires a $1500 DAILY minimum balance and/or a direct deposit of $250 once a month going into the account.

I can only use Southern New Mexico as the place to make my point here, but $1500 in a bank account is asking A LOT from these folks, primarily Hispanic, to keep in the account here. That is every day. If it goes to $1499.99, even for one minute, you are getting charged $12 for that month.

The old saying "Banks make money on your money being there" is true, but hell, even if you are a paycheck to paycheck person with $0 in the account, they are making money off you with every debit card swipe you do. So one can say it's double-dipping. If you have a comma in your bank account and have not strayed from having that comma, then it is something that you can't understand because you haven't worked in a bank.

$250/once a month direct deposit? Hard for hundreds of thousands of people of color. Why? Because many people of color work at jobs with no direct deposit. The McDonald's franchisee in this town of 100,000 people doesn't offer direct deposit to his hundreds of employees. My family's restaurant still, to this day, has NEVER offered direct deposit to its employees, despite the best efforts of my mom to push for it.

The owner of my family's restaurant, the Owl Bar & Cafe, is in her 80s, and she and my Uncle will go to their grave before becoming tech-savvy enough to offer that. It's not fear of what's new; it's sticking to what works for them. I had a prominent businessman here in Las Cruces tell me to my face, "I like to personally write every paycheck out to my employees. That's why I don't like that computer stuff."

Well, that is all well and good, if all of his employees, which was near 100 last time I talked to him, all had Bank of America, didn't get direct deposit, and had less than $1500 in their bank account, if they had Advantage Plus at BofA (the primary bank account), they would have paid BofA $14,400 collectively over one year, because the old man's personal gesture flies in the face of BofA's desire not to have repeat clients do basic things like cash checks in their branch. Most of those employees were Spanish speakers.

We can talk about overdraft fees having elements of racism

too, but people who disagree with my points will say it is about "personal responsibility" with those fees. Fair, but when you give a business card to an account holder, saying you'll be there if they need you while pushing them towards the app for everything, you are already saying, "This is a one-night stand. I got what I wanted. Get lost."

To Bank of America's credit, they are lowering overdraft fees in a couple of months from $35 per transaction to $10 per transaction. (37) While this is something to applaud, Capital One is doing away with overdraft fees altogether, on top of the fact that their basic banking is free with no minimums. So if Capital One sees their free banking as a model to grow their business, including their credit card division (We've all seen the MF Samuel L Jackson commercials), why doesn't BofA do the same?

Because the people who get hit with fees are the type of clients BofA, in my opinion, tries to avoid. You know that someone with $10 in their account isn't coming to you for a home loan. You know that a serial overdraft fee-generating client isn't going to go in and invest with Merrill. The reason so many branches are still temporarily closed with BofA in certain areas tells me that it is a byproduct of those areas likely having these clients they can't get deep with for financial reasons, and sad to say that majority of those areas are communities of color.

Since I started my project, there have been multiple BofA closures in the Chicago area. (38) Yes, bank branches close all the time, I understand. However, when you hear that BofA has lent $1.5 Billion in money for home loans in that area and 83.01% of the borrowers are white, and 2.89% are black in a city that I know to be a minimum of half-Black, then we got a problem. How do you explain BofA fawning over their nearly $1 Billion HQ on Wacker Drive while closing branches in the same city (39), just in the more urban neighborhoods?

HIGH-RISK TRANSACTION

Bank of America, plus other banks like Chase and Wells Fargo, which were in that report, are creating these bank deserts where customers are phased out of banking in their city. They do this by eliminating neighborhood branches and leaving open just a few in big cities, all geared mainly towards sales only and not service. You wouldn't build a skyscraper if you were entirely exiting a market. They were just leaving those areas in the market that didn't make them as much money.

That Atlanta branch of Bank of America where Ryan Coogler was put in handcuffs was like that. The manager mentioned she was just assigned to that branch that day. A brief search on Linkedin showed a whole new team at that same branch a month later. Were the others fired? No, but they are going above and beyond to keep a branch that likely generates money open. In contrast, branches mainly just cashing paychecks remain closed in mainly minority-heavy areas "because of COVID."

I did a podcast about an article I read in a Los Angeles-area publication (40) about all the banks in that area mysteriously being "temporarily closed" while others were open and swamped. The area is East LA. East LA is a heavily Hispanic area of that city, for those who don't know. My followers were pissed at the distance to the nearest branch and the wait time they had to deal with just for choosing to bank there.

Customers recognize that switching out associates all the time is terrible as well. They don't develop the relationships they want to have with their bankers. That constant state of flux is more of a problem than anything the teller perceived that Ryan Coogler did in the interaction because she is not given a chance to understand the quirks of certain clients.

I saw the damnedest thing while looking up anything I could about the Bank of America branch where this happened on 1280 Paces Ferry Road. It was a post from Larry Wilkerson, a BofA leader in that area. In a Linkedin post (41) I shared to Twitter from February 2022, Wilkerson posted a photo of the staff inside the very branch Ryan Coogler was arrested in, "Celebrating" Black History Month.

While commendable, the photo has a lot of problems. First off, the post says that the staff is honoring HBSU colleges by wearing the colors of "Moorehouse College," a local Black college in Atlanta.

First off, it's HBCU, short for Historically Black Colleges and Universities. We mix up S and C sometimes as humans. No biggie. But a white manager says that the group is honoring a college that he can't spell correctly (Morehouse). I think it's mildly important for a banker to know the proper spelling of a university that theoretically has a lot of customers you would want into your bank as clients, right?

Secondly, they put the two African-American employees in the front of the picture, which is cringe-worthy. I can hear someone arranging that photo saying, "Hey, since you guys are Black, get in the front of us." When you see it, you will see how weird the pose is.

Thirdly, speaking of poses, a white banker is kneeling for some unknown reason in the photo. Why? What the hell? There's a diminutive female banker behind him that he could easily have gotten behind if trying to cram into the picture was a big deal. But there's plenty of space, even with social distancing, as there are people closer than he would be to anyone.

So I think the kneeling is on purpose. I have absolutely nothing against it at all. It's your right to do what you feel is right for your beliefs, but it's so bizarre to see him kneeling, a pose synonymous with racial injustice, when the two African-American employees are standing like they are just taking a picture.

I know I am likely overthinking the fuck out of this picture, but its optics are just bizarre. You are celebrating a college you can't spell by wearing their colors? How about just treating Black clients better? When a photo leaves you with more questions than answers, you can tell it was poorly thought out.

I blocked the faces, but check it out with the provided link.

One of the most striking things I have covered while doing my Notorious Banker project is a story done in St. Louis, MO, just before COVID. The local CBS affiliate did a story on people in a 90+ % Black neighborhood complaining that BofA closed their ATMs at a particular branch at 6 pm. (42) I couldn't believe it. It just blew my mind that a community, which likely has many workers working non-traditional hours already at demanding jobs, did not have access to their own money at their bank at the only times they had time to access it.

Bank of America cited "security reasons" for those early closures. Okay, but why have I heard the same things from people in Tampa, the Crenshaw District of Los Angeles, and Chicago? Because it's not true. There was only one incident of documented robbery at an ATM at that St. Louis branch, and it was not considered a random crime. The victim and perp knew each other.

The news station KMOV no longer has it on its website, but it is still on YouTube. I wonder if BofA pressured them to remove that story because I had a hell of a time finding it.

Robberies happen everywhere; it doesn't matter the day and time. It is bound to happen, but you can't stop business because of the fear of something happening, you know? The craziest fucking thing about that particular BofA closing its ATMs early was the location of the nearest location with 24-hour ATMs. The customers in the primarily Black neighborhood would have to cross through the Ferguson neighborhood, a city synonymous with racial unrest after the killing of Michael Brown there by police officers in 2014.

I am not from a big city, but I know most who live in big cities don't go traipsing around the whole city every day unless that's their job. So for BofA having clients go long distances to access ATMs makes it seem similar to how Texas is trying to make it hard for people of color to vote by having one polling location per city. I know what some of you are saying. "Just go to the ATM at the store." I get that. I do. But it will hit you with fees, taking away more money that these folks so desperately need, not to mention that the bank hits you with an out-of-network fee. It's forcing you to leave.

Let me just say a personal observation here before I continue (Like I wasn't going to tell it anyway)...

I think BofA spends WAYYYYYY too much time trying to show the world how not racist they are by philanthropy only and not in how they interact with clients of color. Now, I will never fault a company for giving money to good causes. 5 days after George Floyd, BofA announced a comprehensive 4 year/$1 Billion initiative to address economic and racial inequality. (43)

The crazy people on the right saw that commitment and believed it was a donation to BLM to riot in the streets. So stupid. The money was for COVID testing, grants to colleges and museums, and so many things that touch the lives of people of color.

Let me be the first to commend that and applaud them for giving these much-needed things some attention while other companies also did well. It was important and needed to be done. The timing of less than a week after George Floyd's killing was a little weird, to be honest, but again, It's fantastic that they did that.

But here's the fucking kicker of why I think they are trying too hard. In March of 2021, there was a spree killing of six Asian women in the Atlanta area, the site of the Coogler arrest. Eight people in total were murdered. The reasons for the killing of these poor women in the massage parlors of Atlanta were just too fucked up that I don't want to discuss it here. Look it up. (44)

Asian American violence is sad, and since the pandemic, we have seen an uptick of hate going that way, and it is just wrong. So what does Bank of America do a couple of days after the incident of mass murder? They change the cover photo on their social media pages to a stock photo of an Asian woman on her computer, presumably banking. (45)

It was so just bizarre. I had to chuckle to myself. I imagined the bank's social media team spending a couple of days brainstorming on the most potent way to boast about their JD Power Award-Winning Online Banking (By the way, you have to pay JD Power to say you are a JD Power Award Winner) (46) and honor Asians that passed away at the same time?

Oh, let's use a stock photo of an Asian woman that would generally appear in our advertising in the branch to honor these people. You can't make this up.

Two weeks after the killing, they added $250 million to their $1 Billion commitment and changed the commitment from 4 years to 5 years to address economic and racial inequality. (47) This press release made me pose a question in my head.

"Does that mean every race is worth $250,000,000 to them?"

While I am happy that they are giving to worthy Asian institutions, all listed on the press release, I find the timing distasteful. Were they NOT going to give this money to Asian non-profits before the mass murder in Atlanta or not? Why did they hold out nearly a year to include them when they could have done so in the June 2020 announcement? Why is the quote in the press release from Thong Nguyen, Vice Chairman at Bank of America? You get the highest-ranking Asian man in your company to use his Asian heritage as a backdrop for your commitment that you easily could have done before 8 people died. Why do they try so hard to show how forward-thinking they are when incidents like Coogler, where race is a factor that happens to customers of color, happen often?

In my opinion, in some bizarre way of thinking, these donations are a way to advertise their services. They consider it an investment in growing their company because in June 2020 and in March and April of 2021, literally every bot Twitter account I saw tweeting about BofA discussed this giving, along with many news stations both locally and nationally. It's weird and pandering in the face of tragedy. Why wait until something horrible happens to someone of color before you give and make a big deal about it?

Again, I do not hate giving. Give as much as you want, BofA. Your timing fucking sucks, though.

I do believe one element that impacted Coogler has roots in discriminating against people of color. That is the "high-risk" alert for a large cash withdrawal. Not the >$10k CTR. I get that's a federal thing. I am talking about the red box message described by the teller, seen by me when it was introduced during my time at Bank of America and was the catalyst for the freak out by the teller here.

So, I am Mexican-American and grew up around a massively Hispanic community. We like cash for some reason. We like it more than cards. We will take less money selling something if it means getting cash. I have seen hundreds of people sell their "food stamp" benefits on a card at a rate of $3 in food for every $1 in cash. I know it's illegal, but honestly, it's part of my ingrained culture.

Most African-Americans I worked with, had as clients, or interacted with prefer cash over anything. I had a ton of Chinese students at my bank. Though the Chinese are most adept at using NFC Technology to make payments than Americans, the average student would open an account with $5-$10k in crisp $100 bills. Ditto the Saudi, Kuwaiti and Korean Students I had.

Nothing wrong with that. It's a personal preference. How does BofA drop the ball with cash? Because I mentioned earlier in the book that in an interview with Fox Business a couple of years ago, CEO Brian Moynihan mentioned a cost of $5 Billion a year for "moving cash all around the country," indicating that ordering cash from the feds, transport, hiring armored cars. All of that is very expensive, and they were looking to trim that expense.

When I was still there, the amount of money we could buy into the bank for a busy day was lessened, as were the number of times the armored car came to help us by bringing or shipping out money for us. The limiting of getting cash into the bank limits the number of people that can be helped like Ryan Coogler wanted to be helped, so that is why that red box warning is there.

It's as much a way not to help that person as it is to "protect the account." The referral to the manager, who is likely much more skilled at BS than the teller, is part of it, and I have seen times, hell, I have been there during times where we flat out refused to do a transaction for no other reason that we didn't have the money on hand. We didn't tell them that, though. We gave them an option of a cashier's check, which required no cash or to go to the ATM if it was a lower amount because that money in the ATM falls in another bucket than the branch cash.

The shitty thing? Even in my old branch, we chose where to

make exceptions. I wasn't on that side of the bank when those red box warnings happened, but I know we decided who we "should" help with getting money without a problem and who we should "suggest" other ways of banking to. Though we are all Hispanic, we discriminated against clients we favored over others. It sucks. It does.

I didn't see it as discriminatory until I left, got my project started, and saw these incidents of refusal by bank employees to help clients repeatedly on social media, and then it all made sense.

At the beginning of this book, I mentioned that Bank of America closed a branch near the Navajo Nation in Gallup, NM. So many Natives banked at BofA, I can attest that it was the busiest branch in the state, even busier than the ones in Albuquerque, with 20x the population.

Gallup, NM probably has 7 in 10 folks there fluent in Navajo. BofA used to put "Navajo speaking preferred" in their job listings. It was that important to help service the clientele, right? Nah. They wanted Navajo speakers to see if there were any potential sales of credit cards or auto loans in this group of folks, the majority of which likely don't even clear $10k a year.

When the time was announced to go and close that branch, a simple Tiktok video by me led to thousands of Natives sharing it. Their outrage at the bank leaving, knowing that in a world of expensive fuel, families where elders don't drive and abject poverty, the nearest branches being 2 hours away and the closest ATM is 45 minutes away is far from convenient.

It was a way of ridding thousands of people by suffocating the easy access to their federal deposits and creating a bank desert as big as the desert southwest itself. I spent the better part of 3 months answering emails and phone calls about other banks in their area that they should move to, and I gave my honest opinion and helped as much as I could, being 5 hours away.

It led me to a new reality where I will be talking about these issues as my full-time job and helping people get into banks that are comfy for them without me being tied to any institutions. It's work that someone's got to do. I have increased my Tiktok following 5 fold since the closure announcement and this Ryan Coogler story. People care about these things.

New York Times Reporter Emily Flitter is writing a book about racism in banking (48) that will be more polished and awesome than a book I write could ever be. I am not a journalist. I am just a guy who listens to people. It's coming out in October 2022, and I am excited about it. I will read it, and depending on the book's content, I may have an entire BofA racism book to talk about with interactions from many of my followers who found me after their battles with being discriminated against there. If her book hits all the notes from my already written book, I will pivot to other book opportunities about my time in banking that are important to me, as long as the message gets across.

Racism in banking is real. It manifests itself in many ways. I hope I have shown that to you in this chapter and understand where I am coming from and why I had to write this book.

FINALLY

I had a night to sleep on this chapter. My team, The NM State Aggies won a big game in the NCAA Tournament last night, and I was on such a high, I wrote until 2:30 in the morning. I could have stayed up all night. I am glad I got 5 hours of sleep, though, because it allowed me this nice, fluffy thought in my head that made me feel better about why I am writing this.

Many people follow my content on social media and see that I am harsh toward my former company and Wells Fargo. Why? There's documented history of them fucking up royally and fucking customers over royally. Everyone knows that besides those in banking. Fake accounts? Bailout money? These are things we know. Through my project, I've learned that many employees at my former company and other big banks feel this way but say nothing. Why?

It is because the employees are afraid of repercussions. Simple as that. I always said the "ethics compliance" hotline at Bank of America should be renamed the "fast track to being fired" hotline. The stakes are too big for some person to report something bad they saw or something the bank is doing that they feel icky about and want to tell someone. Fuck that, fire them, let them sue, and maybe we will pay them out. Let's continue to make our billions. That's the Bobby Axelrod *Billions* approach.

Me? I was born poor. I am not rich now, and money doesn't drive me as it does them. I have a full belly (I'm a very svelte 300lbs, though I lift weights regularly), and my bills are paid. I donate blood plasma to supplement my income, plus I write, and I find ways to make money on social media, helping people in need with their financial institutions. I recently graduated into workplace advocacy and saved 6 jobs in my hometown of Socorro, NM, by helping staff organize and have discussions with their boss on his plan to reduce roles at a medical taxi company.

As much shit as I talk, and trust me, this book is a lot of smack talk. I sincerely think that not only Bank of America should be not mad about it, but they should also commend me for something they used to tell me all the time working there. Over the years, every person who was my boss said to us that "Bank of America believes in 360-degree coaching."

"You shouldn't be afraid to coach. You are here to make us all better."

It's all bullshit because there was never a moment where I had a boss accept critique the way they claim was allowed by us to make our centers better. I once sent an email to a regional manager of mine, Lonnie, a man I liked a lot from the time he gifted me a sandwich at my first branch in Socorro, NM, in the Mid-2000s.

At one point in time, I was concerned about how many people from Holloman AFB in Alamogordo, NM, were coming to my branch an hour away and complaining. They were groaning that not only were bank branches not available on the base, but BofA had ended its relationship with Valero Gas Stations to have their ATMs there, and soon enough, all the ATMs were gone from that town. According to me, saying to my smart speaker, "Hey, Google, how many active-duty people are at Holloman AFB?" (great source, right?), the number was 21,000. It seemed like I had 100 people complain to just me in one month.

So, I wrote Lonnie, letting him know my concern about these complaints because theoretically, they would impact our customer service score, which influenced our performance reviews. I said, "Is there some way I can propose to talk to someone in a higher office at BofA about the need for at least installing one ATM back in Alamogordo?" I was genuine about it, not trying to make a power play because I used those ATMs too on trips. I was just looking to help.

To his credit, Lonnie sent me this note saying (I'm paraphrasing), "James, thanks for the email. I hear your concerns, and I can forward them up the chain. We are always finding ways to maximize our business, and things like that are fluid. Thanks for all that you do for Amador." He was a good guy. Bank of America shipped him off to work at WaFd after selling many branches to them, including the first branch I worked at in 2005.

It was a nice note. It meant a lot to be heard in a company of 204,000 people. Whether he sent a letter up the chain or not was irrelevant because a couple of days later, my branch manager got wind that I sent an email to Lonnie and "broke the chain of command." Meaning that I shouldn't talk to Lonnie without using her as a vessel to speak to him, as if she was Joseph Smith who founded the LDS religion and she can see only the words of God and is the only vessel to communicate something important. I was told that was not an acceptable thing by me, and going forward, don't send any unsolicited emails to people who are not your direct boss.

What the hell? I was just tired of buff military men going to me and my branch saying, "I HATE YOUR FUCKING BANK!!! I HAVE TO DRIVE AN HOUR TO BANK NOW!!!". If anything, knowing how AFBs and other military installations work, I would figure BofA would see it as helping those people currently there and future potential clients who transfer into the base.

Whatever, it doesn't matter anymore. My point is anytime I sincerely tried to help my team and company with suggestions that they claimed was not only welcomed but encouraged, I would get smacked down like that about breaking some unwritten rule about stepping too high up the ladder to be heard.

I shared this story because I see this Ryan Coogler incident as a teaching moment for Bank of America. One that I know goddamn well will not be in their onboarding training, nor any refreshers tenured employees will have, save for the people involved in this who didn't get fired. In my mind, BofA should be proud that they taught me to analyze things, know policy and employee roles, and pinpoint what went wrong.

Of course, my findings will lead to pointing the finger at the bank as a whole, which I am sure they will hate, but that's on them. They should want to learn not to arrest prominent Black people trying to do the most basic transactions. The bigger problem is why do they make transactions like that so difficult?

Because BofA is trying to rebrand itself the same way Champion athletic wear is rebranding itself as a boutique brand all the kids love. Ten years ago, you saw Champion in the clearance rack at Walmart, and now those same clothes are going for premium rates. BofA wants to be the brand for wealth, not overdraft-fee-ridden clients.

They don't want to be the Walmart of banking, servicing millions of clients. They would rather have 1 client with a $5 Million average balance than 50,000 with a $100 average balance because those 50,000, you have to build branches for, buy TP for the bathrooms in those branches, train and retain staff, lease a building, pay the electric bill, etc.

Not to mention that those clients are the ones holding up your lines, complaining about overdraft fees and monthly fees, and the lack of staff in your branch. They will never grow into clients needing more from their bank. But if you have 1 guy and train him to only come to you when he needs something that will help your goals, you've won if you are BofA.

Ryan Coogler was the rich man, and he was the man who needed to stand in line. He was both of those types of clients rolled up into one, and that's not a bad thing. He required service, and as a preferred client, he knew it should be easy to get it done. That is until it wasn't easy, and it ended up being a horrible day.

You can blame the teller and the managers all you want for this, and rightfully so, but you also have to blame the bank. The bank is the one who hired these people to be timeshare people in a bank where ⅔ of the people I talk to on social media ever realize that the main reason a branch exists is sales.

Ever go to Vegas and deal with those aggressive-ass timeshare people asking you how long you are staying in Vegas? It's the worst kind of salesman. My wife and I can spot them from 50 yards away, and we unlock our hands and walk apart because they usually hound the shit out of married couples. It sucks. Bank of America has become that while sacrificing the focus on any good service whatsoever.

The branch manager's focus? Sales. The assistant manager's focus? Compliance. The teller's focus? Referrals of customers to bankers for sales purposes. Who's in charge of servicing the clients with basic bank transactions. Wait, what's that?

The focus is long gone from Bank of America to help people do what most think are the only things that matter at a bank, which is depositing and withdrawing cash and getting a lollipop for your little one. (Fun fact, My BofA region forbade us from ordering lollies a couple of years before I left. My coworkers and I probably spent $200 on them out of pocket to keep clients happy because BofA is so damn cheap)

But I wrote this book in a week because it is so easy to talk about this subject when you have immersed yourself in a job for the better part of a decade, and you listened to your training and did the best you could in a bad situation. In a way, I feel bad for those at the branch where the Ryan Coogler incident happened because they were never trained to be at their best. They were trained to make it look like they knew how to run a bank so that, you know, they could get more sales.

I mentioned earlier in the book that I sincerely apologize to Ryan Coogler for this incident happening and for having to write a book about it. But like a movie director putting all elements of a movie together to make their artistic point, I used this incident to prove a point I have been screaming about for 4 years. Things like this will happen again—Mark my words. Bank of America will hope you forget about the Ryan Coogler incident. I never will, and if I wrote this book well enough, you would never forget it either.

Thank You.

EPILOGUE

What I have discussed in the book is something that I immerse myself in every day. Although I am no longer working for a specific bank, and have my biases towards companies that harm clients, I discussed what I feel in this book in the hopes that things change for the better.

My commitment to everyone is I intend of being a part of the good change in this industry through my writing, commentary, and my hard work through my consumer advocacy. I love to help people, and this book is a step towards helping more.

I encourage you to check out my social media channels, whether it be
Tiktok **(@NotoriousBanker)**,
Instagram **(@NotoriousBanker)**,
Twitter **(@BankBetterGuy)** and interact with me and others about the things that bother you with banks.

You can also email me at thenotoriousbanker@gmail.com
Leave a voicemail at (575) 322-4127

Contribute to my project via CashApp - $TheNotoriousBanker
Venmo - TheNotoriousBanker
Subscribe monthly at Patreon.com/NotoriousBanker
Or by mail at the address below:

The Notorious Banker
PO BOX 14214
Las Cruces, NM 88013

ACKNOWLEDGEMENT

Thanks to my wife, Gabrielle for being supportive of my project.

Thanks to all the brave employees of big banks I talk to off the record every single day to glimpse into the world I love but never want to go back to.

Thanks to all the followers on my social media, 5 Million Views on Tiktok, 4 Million Impressions on Twitter in the last month alone! You are spreading the word and interacting with my content, and I just love that so much!

Thanks to those of you who contribute weekly/monthly to my project to keep me working hard to help others.

Thanks to the reporters I talk to on a near-regular basis. You make me feel like these stories need to be told, and I will be there for you when you want me to tell them more and more.

Thanks to the ex-coworkers I learned a lot from, good and bad. I always say, "I couldn't have sucked if I worked at a place 13 years." I wouldn't have lasted without the lessons learned from those people.

Thanks to all the content creators whose content I referenced and linked to in this book project. You make me smarter and keep me entertained and informed.

ABOUT THE AUTHOR

James Baca - The Notorious Banker

James Baca is a writer, consumer and workplace advocate, podcast host, and content creator. He is known professionally as "The Notorious Banker"

James created "The Notorious Banker" in 2018, after 13 years at Bank of America in various roles up to sales manager. TNB helps people understand bank policy and helps clients escalate issues properly to their banks for further assistance. James has recovered over $2 Million in fees.

With TNB's workplace advocacy, James helps people understand their rights in the workforce by helping people interpret state labor laws and coordinating how employees can properly file grievances with their company or the state departments of labor.

"The Notorious Banker Podcast" available on all platforms is straight acerbic commentary about issues in the banking industry that impact the general retail banking public. TNB reaches 4,000-9,000 downloads per podcast.

James is active on social media, achieving 3-5 million views on Tiktok per month, and 2-4 million impressions on Twitter per month, as of March 2022.

"High-Risk Transaction" is James' 7th book, but 2nd under his real name. James has been married to his wife Gabrielle since 2014, and currently resides in Las Cruces, NM. Originally from Socorro, NM, He is a 2008 Graduate of Eastern New Mexico University.

BOOKS BY THIS AUTHOR

Please Try Your Call Again Later

Please Try Your Call Again Later is my story of fighting like hell for assistance that was allegedly available to everyone during the COVID-19 Pandemic. Like many people, COVID-19 impacted my income severely, and brought my work as a consumer advocate to a standstill. Stimulus money, PPP loans, and child tax credits kept many afloat during this time. Amended rules allowed me to apply for unemployment benefits. More than 18 months later, I am at a stalemate to be fully approved.

I have called over a thousand times to the New Mexico Department of Workforce Solutions (NMDWS) just to be hung up on. According to media reports, The State of New Mexico at one point was only answering 6% of calls! The three times I connected with an associate only led to additional issues to my application. Help has never seemed so far away.

The experience I have endured has eerie parallels to the customer service ineptitude of the banking industry, which I worked in for 13 years. I explain that while we applauded companies for stepping up customer service during the first part of COVID-19, the foot is definitely off the gas pedal now.

This book details every insane step made by me asking for help, as well as every insane misstep made by the state. I share my stories of interacting with an outdated website, and an overworked, overwhelmed apathetic staff at NMDWS. I also discuss how this experience has shown me how the less fortunate are left behind and ridiculed for asking for help, which in turn has changed my mindset to be a person who gives back to the community that gave me success. I also get personal and discuss the health and financial hurdles NMDWS has thrown my way by screwing up my case and the cases of others.

It's a story you never believe can happen to you…Until it happens to you.

If the state doesn't want to pay me the money rightfully available to me by law, then, what the hell? Let's write a book about how awful they have been to me and others, sell it for a fair price, make that money back, and give some of it to great causes as a unique way of sticking it to the man!

www.ingramcontent.com/pod-product-compliance
Lightning Source LLC
Chambersburg PA
CBHW071505220526
45472CB00003B/919